NTSB/RAR-10/01
PB2010-916301
Notation 8175
Adopted January 21, 2010

I0417189

Railroad Accident Report

Collision of Metrolink Train 111 With
Union Pacific Train LOF65-12
Chatsworth, California
September 12, 2008

**National
Transportation
Safety Board**

490 L'Enfant Plaza, S.W.
Washington, D.C. 20594

National Transportation Safety Board. 2010. *Collision of Metrolink Train 111 With Union Pacific Train LOF65–12, Chatsworth, California, September 12, 2008*. Railroad Accident Report NTSB/RAR-10/01. Washington, DC.

Abstract: About 4:22 p.m., Pacific daylight time, on Friday, September 12, 2008, westbound Southern California Regional Rail Authority Metrolink train 111, consisting of one locomotive and three passenger cars, collided head-on with eastbound Union Pacific Railroad (UP) freight train LOF65–12 near Chatsworth, California. The Metrolink train derailed its locomotive and lead passenger car; the UP train derailed its 2 locomotives and 10 of its 17 cars. The force of the collision caused the locomotive of train 111 to telescope into the lead passenger coach by about 52 feet. The accident resulted in 25 fatalities, including the engineer of train 111. Emergency response agencies reported transporting 102 injured passengers to local hospitals. Damages were estimated to be in excess of $12 million.

Contents

Figures

Acronyms and Abbreviations

BMI   body mass index

CFR   *Code of Federal Regulations*

Connex   Connex Railroad, LLC

CP   control point

FRA   Federal Railroad Administration

GPS   global positioning system

HIV   human immunodeficiency virus

NTSB   National Transportation Safety Board

OSA   obstructive sleep apnea

SCRRA   Southern California Regional Rail Authority

UP   Union Pacific Railroad

Executive Summary

About 4:22 p.m., Pacific daylight time, on Friday, September 12, 2008, westbound Southern California Regional Rail Authority Metrolink train 111, consisting of one locomotive and three passenger cars, collided head-on with eastbound Union Pacific Railroad freight train LOF65–12 near Chatsworth, California. The Metrolink train derailed its locomotive and lead passenger car; the UP train derailed its 2 locomotives and 10 of its 17 cars. The force of the collision caused the locomotive of train 111 to telescope into the lead passenger coach by about 52 feet. The accident resulted in 25 fatalities, including the engineer of train 111. Emergency response agencies reported transporting 102 injured passengers to local hospitals. Damages were estimated to be in excess of $12 million.

The National Transportation Safety Board determines that the probable cause of the September 12, 2008, collision of a Metrolink commuter train and a Union Pacific freight train was the failure of the Metrolink engineer to observe and appropriately respond to the red signal aspect at Control Point Topanga because he was engaged in prohibited use of a wireless device, specifically text messaging, that distracted him from his duties. Contributing to the accident was the lack of a positive train control system that would have stopped the Metrolink train short of the red signal and thus prevented the collision.

The safety issues identified during this accident investigation are as follows:

- Inadequate capability, because of the privacy offered by a locomotive operating compartment, for management to monitor crewmember adherence to operating rules such as those regarding the use of wireless devices or the presence of unauthorized persons in the operating compartment.

- Lack of a positive train control system on the Metrolink rail system.

As a result of its investigation of this accident, the National Transportation Safety Board makes recommendations to the Federal Railroad Administration.

Factual Information

Accident Synopsis

About 4:22 p.m., Pacific daylight time,[1] on Friday, September 12, 2008, westbound Southern California Regional Rail Authority (SCRRA) Metrolink train 111, consisting of one locomotive and three passenger cars, collided head-on with eastbound Union Pacific Railroad (UP) freight train LOF65–12 near Chatsworth, California. The Metrolink train derailed its locomotive and lead passenger car; the UP train derailed its 2 locomotives and 10 of its 17 cars. The force of the collision caused the locomotive of train 111 to telescope into the lead passenger coach by about 52 feet. The accident resulted in 25 fatalities, including the engineer of train 111. Emergency response agencies reported transporting 102 injured passengers to local hospitals. Damages were estimated to be in excess of $12 million.

Accident Narrative

At 5:54 a.m. on the morning of the accident, the two-member crew (conductor and engineer) who were aboard Metrolink train 111 at the time of the accident reported for duty at the Metrolink crew base in Montalvo, California. Once on duty, the crew participated in a job briefing where they discussed track warrants and bulletins from the various territories over which they would be operating that day. The crew departed the yard eastbound[2] about 6:45 a.m. aboard train 106. The train made 10 station stops before arriving at Los Angeles Union Station at 8:25 a.m. (See figure 1.) At 8:32 a.m. the crewmembers took the train a few miles west to Metrolink's central maintenance facility, where they went off duty at 9:26 a.m. The conductor said he then went upstairs to the "quiet" room provided for employees and that the engineer, as was his usual practice during the mid-day relief,[3] drove home.

At 11:30 a.m. the three-member crew (engineer, conductor, and brakeman) of UP freight train LOF65–12 (hereinafter referred to as the Leesdale Local) reported for duty in Gemco, California. The Leesdale Local departed Gemco westbound at 12:30 p.m. with orders to service local industries along the route.

The Metrolink train crew returned to duty at the central maintenance facility at 2:00 p.m. The conductor said the engineer spoke of having gotten a 2-hour nap during the mid-day break. The crew participated in a job briefing and was issued new track bulletins. They then traveled to the yard, boarded the equipment scheduled for train 111—which consisted of one locomotive,

---

[1] Unless otherwise noted, all times in this report are Pacific daylight time.

[2] Unless otherwise noted, directions referred to in this report are railroad timetable directions, which often differ from compass direction.

[3] The Metrolink train crew worked split shifts. They operated trains during the morning and afternoon rush periods and were off during the middle of the day.

two regular passenger cars, and one passenger coach/cab control car[4]—and departed at 3:03 p.m. in non-revenue service from the maintenance facility to Union Station, arriving at 3:12:03 p.m.

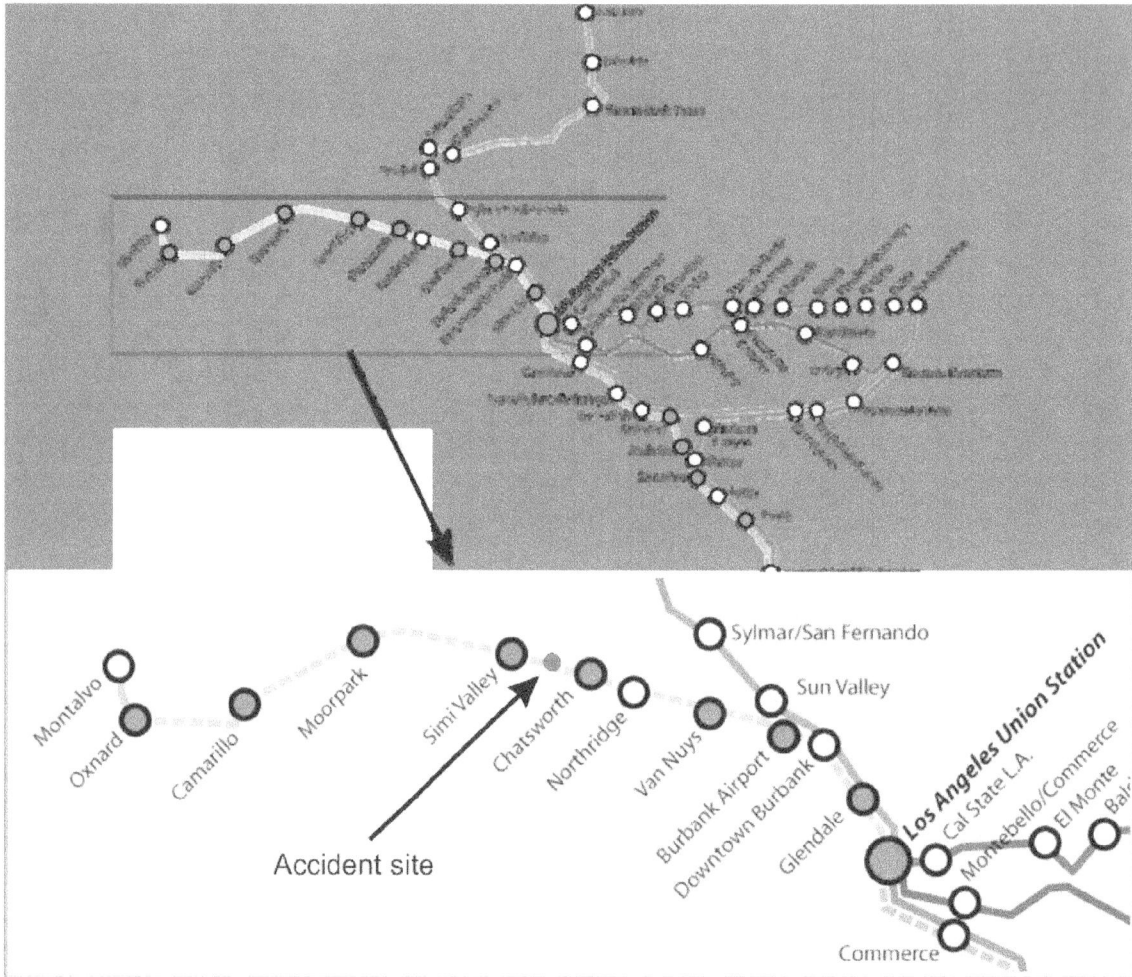

Figure 1. The accident occurred on Metrolink's Ventura Subdivision, about 33 miles west of Los Angeles.

Verizon Wireless records of calls and text messages to and from the engineer's personal cell phone/wireless device showed that while the engineer was en route from the maintenance facility to Union Station he received a text message from an individual who will be referred to in this report as "Person A."[5] This was the first of seven text messages Person A transmitted to the engineer from the time train 111 departed the maintenance facility until the accident.

---

[4] The trains operated by the crew on the day of the accident were commuter trains configured in a "push-pull" arrangement that allows the train to operate in either direction without being turned. In the "pull" mode, the engineer operates from the locomotive at the head end of the train. In the "push" mode, the locomotive is at the rear of the train and the engineer occupies the operating compartment of a cab control car (a specially configured passenger coach) that, in the push mode, is at the head end of the train. At the time of this accident, the train was operating in the pull mode, and the engineer was in the locomotive at the head end.

[5] As will be discussed later in this report, the engineer had, earlier in the day, exchanged a number of text messages with the individual identified as Person A.

While train 111 was at Union Station and before it began its westbound trip, the engineer received the second text message from Person A. The records indicated that the engineer responded with two text messages to Person A, the first sent at 3:23:59 p.m. and the next at 3:30:49 p.m.[6] These were the first of six text messages the engineer would transmit to Person A that afternoon. At 3:21:42 p.m. and again at 3:26:11 p.m., the engineer made two cell phone calls, each lasting 75 seconds, to two different phone numbers (neither of them belonging to Person A). These were the only voice calls the engineer made while he was on duty on the afternoon of the accident.

Meanwhile, the Leesdale Local had completed its westbound work assignments at Oxnard, California, and, at 3:13 p.m., had begun its eastbound return trip to Gemco, which is near the Metrolink Van Nuys station. The Leesdale Local departed Oxnard with two locomotive units pulling 17 cars. For this return trip, the engineer and the conductor were in the lead locomotive while the brakeman rode the trailing unit.

Train 111 departed Los Angeles Union Station westbound on schedule at 3:34:54 p.m.[7] en route to Moorpark, California. The engineer occupied the locomotive at the head end of the train, and the conductor was in the last passenger car. The train would be operating on double main line track until reaching Control Point (CP)[8] Raymer (located between the Van Nuys and Northridge stations), where the main line became single track. About 1 minute into the trip, the engineer received the third text message from Person A.

Train 111's first two scheduled stops were Glendale and Downtown Burbank. As the train pulled away from the Downtown Burbank station, at 3:51:08, the Verizon network logged the transmission of the engineer's third text message to Person A. The engineer received the fourth text message from Person A while en route between the Burbank–Bob Hope Airport and Van Nuys stations, and the fifth while en route between the Van Nuys and Northridge stations.

At this time, eastbound Amtrak train 784 was operating on the single track portion of the mainline and on the same track as train 111. The Metrolink dispatcher[9] had aligned switches to route the Amtrak train onto the adjacent main line track at CP Raymer to allow the two trains to pass. Because the switch at CP Raymer was aligned for the eastbound Amtrak train's movement and against any westbound movement, the signal at the control point showed a red aspect, a *stop* indication, for train 111. Metrolink's operations center radio recordings captured the train 111

---

[6] In this report, all times associated with the sending or receiving of calls and text messages are from Verizon records. In these records, the "sent" and "received" times are based on a GPS time reference and reflect the time the Verizon Wireless network equipment either receives or delivers a message. Thus, the reported "sent" time of a message does not necessarily correlate to the time the sender pressed the "send" button on the wireless device. Because the network must query the receiving device to make sure it is available before transmitting a message, the "received" time is more likely to reflect the actual time the message arrives on the recipient's device.

[7] In this report, all times associated with signal, switch, and locomotive events are based on signal log and locomotive event recorder data synchronized to a GPS reference time. This synchronization correlates train position, data recorder, signal, and cell phone send/receive times to a common "master clock" that reflects actual GPS time.

[8] A *control point* is a signal or a siding or crossover switch that is under the control of the dispatcher and that the dispatcher uses to manage train movements over the territory.

[9] The dispatcher referred to in this report was responsible for all train movements over the territory extending from Glendale to Moorpark.

engineer calling this signal ("all red Raymer").[10] After servicing the Van Nuys station, train 111 stopped short of the CP Raymer signal at 4:06:54 to wait for the Amtrak train to move to the other track and for the signal to clear for continued westbound movement. The wait lasted about 3 minutes, during which Verizon records show that the train 111 engineer transmitted the fourth and fifth of his six text messages to Person A. At the end of the stop, the engineer was recorded calling "back in green" (*clear*) at Raymer.

About 2 minutes after train 111 departed CP Raymer, at 4:11 p.m., the eastbound Leesdale Local entered the single track mainline (the same track as train 111) at CP Davis traveling at a recorded speed of 46.6 mph. The dispatcher had aligned the switches so that the eastbound local would enter the 11,300-foot-long controlled siding at CP Topanga, just west of the Chatsworth station. (See figure 2.) The signal circuitry was designed such that, with this switch aligned for the siding, the westbound signal at CP Topanga could not display any aspect other than red (*stop* indication) for westbound trains entering the block of track[11] governed by that signal. This indication required that train 111 stop short of CP Topanga until the Leesdale Local was safely in the siding. Once the train was in the siding, the switch would be realigned for westbound movement on the main line, the signal would be cleared, and train 111 could proceed.[12] Signal data logs showed that the switch at CP Topanga was reversed (aligned for the siding) at 4:07:37 p.m.

Train 111 arrived at Northridge station at 4:14:10 p.m. and departed 40 seconds later. Normal travel time between the Northridge and Chatsworth stations is about 6 minutes. The conductor of train 111 stated that after the train departed Northridge, he began walking through the train. Dispatching center recordings showed that, after departing Raymer, the train 111 engineer called the next three intermediate signals as "green." The next signal the train encountered was the signal at CP Bernson (milepost 446.8), for which Metrolink's operations center recorded the train 111 engineer calling a flashing yellow aspect (*advance approach*). Under an *advance approach* signal indication, trains are to "proceed prepared to stop at second signal." In this case, the second signal was the signal at CP Topanga, where train 111 was to stop and wait for the Leesdale Local to clear the main line. The train passed the CP Bernson signal at 4:17:45 p.m. at a recorded speed of 68 mph. Under Metrolink rules, the conductor of a train must repeat back over the radio any restrictive signal (an indication other than *clear*) called out by the engineer. Train 111's conductor was not recorded repeating back the flashing yellow signal the engineer called at CP Bernson. The conductor said he did not recall hearing the engineer call this signal. A few seconds after train 111's engineer was recorded calling out the flashing yellow aspect at CP Bernson, the engineer of the Leesdale Local was recorded calling out a "green" aspect at CP Davis. Signal data logs showed that this signal had cleared at 4:10:59 p.m.

---

[10] Metrolink operating rules require that engineers announce over the radio the aspects or indications of all wayside signals the train encounters. For an announcement of any signal more restrictive than green (*clear*), the conductor must repeat back the announcement over the radio.

[11] A *block* is a length of track of defined limits, the movement over which is governed by wayside signal indications

[12] As will be discussed later in this report, the commands by the dispatcher to effect these actions had already been "stacked," or entered into the dispatching system at the Metrolink Operations Center.

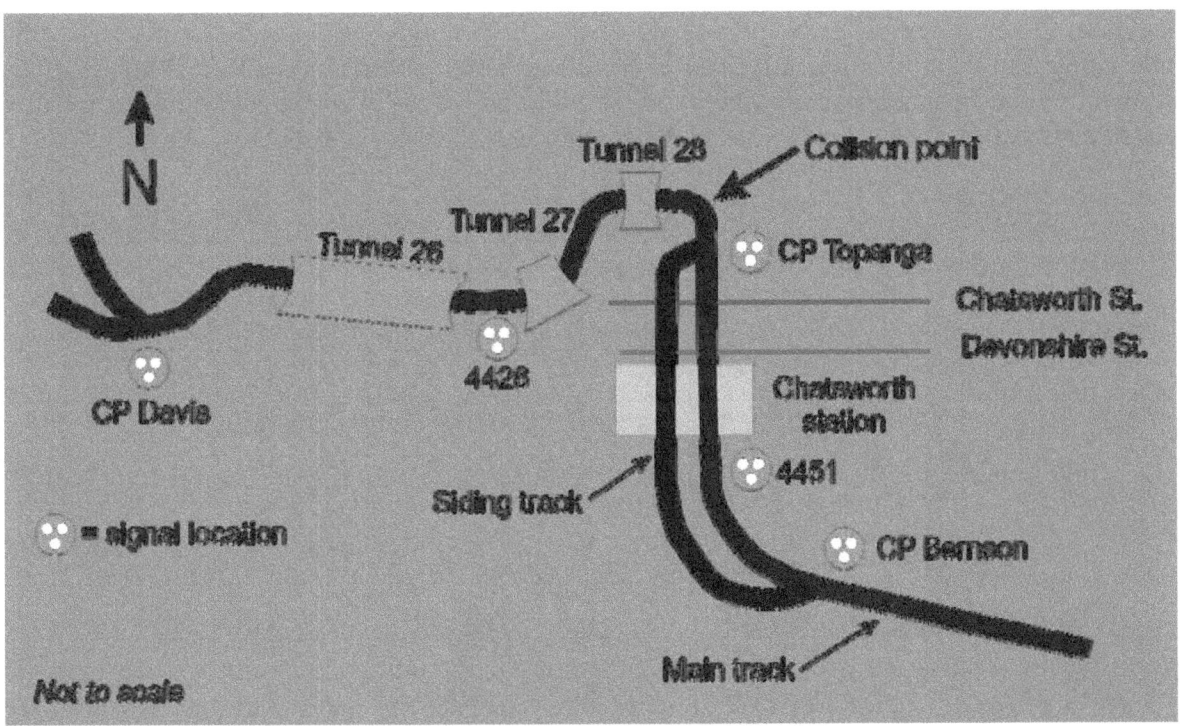

Figure 2. Accident site.

According to signal data logs, the next signal encountered by train 111 after CP Bernson (intermediate signal 4451, just east [geographically south] of the Chatsworth passenger station and the last signal before CP Topanga) was displaying a solid yellow *approach*[13] indication. Train 111 passed signal 4451 at 4:18:41 p.m. Neither the engineer nor the conductor was recorded calling out this signal indication.

At 4:20 p.m., Verizon Wireless network records logged a text message transmitted by the UP conductor from his personal cell phone. At 4:20:15 p.m., a yellow-over-yellow *approach diverging*[14] signal indication displayed at intermediate signal 4426, indicating to the Leesdale Local's crew that their train would be entering the siding at CP Topanga.

Train 111 stopped at Chatsworth station (about 1 mile east [geographically south] of CP Topanga) at 4:19:20 p.m. The stop lasted 57 seconds. The conductor stated that once the train stopped, he opened the train's platform side doors and stepped down from the rear car onto the platform to observe passengers stepping up and down from the train. The conductor stated that his routine was to step back up to at least the first step of the rear passenger car before making the final announcement of the train's impending departure and pressing the buttons to close the doors. He said the door closing sequence takes about 10 seconds, during which time the conductor keeps the door open so he can look down the side of the train. In the first of his three interviews with NTSB investigators, the conductor stated that when he looked forward alongside

---

[13] Under an *approach* indication, trains are to "proceed prepared to stop at the next signal. Trains exceeding 40 MPH must begin reduction to 40 MPH as soon as head end passes signal."

[14] Under an *approach diverging* indication, a train must "proceed prepared to advance on diverging route at next signal not exceeding prescribed speed through turnout(s)."

the train, he could see a green (*clear*) signal at CP Topanga. (See figure 3.) In subsequent interviews, the conductor stated that he had radioed the engineer to "highball 111 on a green signal."[15] Such an announcement was not recorded on any of the available recording devices. He stated that he did not hear a response from the engineer.

Figure 3. CP Topanga as viewed from the cab of a locomotive positioned at Chatsworth station. Upper arrow indicates approximate location of the CP Topanga signal, which is about 5,288 feet away.

Train 111's event recorder showed that at 4:20:07 p.m., the engineer moved the throttle from idle to position 2 and began releasing the train's air brakes. At 4:20:13 p.m., the throttle was moved to position 3. The conductor said that after he closed the crew door, he returned to his desk to update his delay report. He said he had not heard the engineer call any signal since the "green signals departing Northridge on our way to Chatsworth." The data recorder indicated that at 4:20:17 p.m., the brakes were fully released and the train speed was gradually increasing. At 4:20:19 p.m., the throttle was increased to its maximum position of 8, and train speed was 4 mph.

---

[15] As will be discussed later in this report, several other individuals who were on the Chatsworth station platform stated that as train 111 departed the station, they had seen the CP Topanga signal displaying a green aspect.

While departing Chatsworth station, the train remained under the operating authority of the *approach* indication it had received at intermediate signal 4451. Under Metrolink rules, engineers operating under this indication are not to exceed 40 mph while being prepared to stop at the next signal. Additionally, Metrolink's delay-in-block rule (Rule 9.9, discussed later in this report), required engineers, after a station stop,[16] to keep train speeds below 40 mph and be prepared to stop before reaching the next signal, until such time as the next signal can be seen to display a *proceed* indication.

At 4:20:20 p.m., the engineer activated the locomotive bell for 42 seconds. At 4:20:51 p.m., he sounded the locomotive horn for 11 seconds for the Devonshire Road grade crossing. At 4:21:03 p.m., Verizon records show that the engineer received the seventh text message from Person A. At 4:21:23 p.m., the engineer activated the locomotive bell for 19 seconds and also made a short (1 second) sounding of the locomotive horn. While the bell was on, the engineer began sounding the horn at 4:21:34 p.m. for the next crossing at Chatsworth Street. At 4:21:35 p.m. the train's speed was 52 mph. The engineer stopped sounding the horn at 4:21:41 p.m. The train's speed had increased to 54 mph. Over the next 5 seconds, the engineer moved the throttle first to 5, then to 6, back to 5, then to 7, then back to 3 and, finally, to throttle position 4.

At that time, train 111 was about 1,200 feet from the signal at CP Topanga. At 4:21:46 p.m., the engineer initiated a minimum brake pipe pressure reduction that slowed the train. The train passed the CP Topanga signal at 4:21:56 p.m. traveling 44 mph. At 4:22:00 p.m., the engineer released the train's air brakes, and at 4:22:01 p.m., based on the time the transmission was logged as received by the Verizon network, he sent his sixth text message to person A.

According to recorded data for the power-operated switch at CP Topanga (about 377 feet west of the westbound Topanga signal), train 111 ran through the switch at 4:22:02 p.m.[17] At this time, the train's brakes were off and the throttle remained in position 4. A few seconds later, the defect detector just west of the CP Topanga switch broadcast a "no defects" message indicating that train 111 had passed the detector.

On the approach to CP Topanga, the eastbound Leesdale Local traversed two tunnels; the first (tunnel 27) was 924 feet long, and the second (tunnel 28) was 547 feet long. Exiting the second tunnel, the train entered a 6° right-hand curve. According to the Leesdale Local's crewmembers, as their train exited the second tunnel and entered the curve at 40 mph, the Metrolink train came into view. The Leesdale Local's crew activated the train's emergency air braking system, but the trains collided a few seconds later.

The collision occurred at 4:22:23 p.m., about 22 seconds after the Verizon network logged receipt of the engineer's last text message. The point of collision was 634 feet from the east portal of tunnel 28. The event recorder indicated that the train 111 engineer made no change in throttle position or brake application during the 21 seconds that elapsed from the time the train ran through the CP Topanga switch until the collision occurred. Event recorder data indicated

---

[16] The delay-in-block rule applied when a train was delayed for any reason, including a station stop, or whenever train speed had been reduced below 10 mph.

[17] The switch had been aligned for the eastbound Leesdale Local to enter the siding. Train 111 had "run through" the switch from the opposite direction (against this alignment), which damaged the switch components.

that the Metrolink train was traveling about 43 mph and the Leesdale Local was traveling about 41 mph when the two trains collided head-on. (See figure 4.)

Emergency Response

The first 911 call about the accident was received by Los Angeles (City) Fire Department Operations Control Dispatch at 4:23 p.m. from a nearby resident. The dispatch was initially categorized as a "vehic" incident (a physical rescue assignment) but on the basis of numerous additional calls, the incident was upgraded to a "derail" incident, which doubled the resources dispatched.

Figure 4. Overview of accident scene looking south.

The dispatch center requested resources from the Ventura County, Los Angeles County, Culver City, and Beverly Hills fire departments. Los Angeles County Fire Department sent two urban search and rescue teams and helicopters. Ventura County Fire Department sent advanced life support rescues and two squads. Beverly Hills Fire Department and Culver City Fire Department sent rescue squads.

The Los Angeles City Fire Department dispatched the department psychologist, critical response teams, safety officers, and incident management teams. The critical response teams provided family assistance. The incident management teams included fire department officers on special duty, including a rail liaison officer.

The city fire department's operations command was opened to coordinate with the emergency operations center. The general manager of the Emergency Management Division coordinated with different departments of the city to provide long-term logistics such as lighting, food, and water.

Command, Organization, and Resources

The first responding companies were initially dispatched to a residential area near the railroad. The first on-scene captain initially assumed charge of the incident and assigned fire suppression, extrication, and medical tasks. A battalion chief then assumed command when he arrived on scene and remained in charge until the arrival of the assistant chief.

The assistant chief initially established a command post in a school parking lot. When a grassy field adjacent to the command post was selected as a helicopter landing zone, the command post was moved to a parking lot farther away. During the course of the response, the assistant chief established a fire suppression group, an extrication group, and a medical group. A hazardous materials group was established to obtain the train consist and confirm the content of the freight cars.

A unified command system was established with responding agencies. The Los Angeles Police Department was in charge of security and perimeter control. Additional responding agencies were the Los Angeles County Sheriff's Department, Los Angeles County Fire Department, Ventura County Fire Department, Metrolink, Union Pacific, California Office of Emergency Services, the Los Angeles County Coroner, three private ambulance services, and the Red Cross. Los Angeles city agencies that responded were the Department of Transportation, the Department of Public Works, and the Unified School District. Metrolink's chief of safety and security was in charge of Metrolink's response to the accident.

A fence separating the railroad property from the adjacent school was opened to provide access between the trains and the command area. A medical triage area was established next to this fence line. Because of the number of injured passengers, private ambulances were requested to supplement the 28 fire department ambulances. Five air ambulances from Los Angeles Fire Department, the Los Angeles County Fire Department, and the Los Angeles County Sheriff's Department responded. A total of 26 air ambulance flights were conducted. The fire department's medical director responded to the scene, along with two medical "caches" (trailers stocked with medical supplies). During the first 8 hours of the response, the fire department resources included 42 fire companies, 25 ambulances, 8 chief officers, 7 emergency medical services captains, 3 urban search and rescue teams, 5 helicopters, 2 command post units, and 2 communications support units. In total, 350 firefighters (from all fire departments), 150 sheriff's department deputies, and 440 Los Angeles Police Department officers responded. In all, more than 1,000 emergency personnel participated in the response effort.

Extrication Operations

The earliest responders accessed the accident site from the rear yard of a house in the adjacent residential area. The first police officers to arrive on the scene used bolt cutters to cut through the fence and provide access to the accident site.

Leesdale Local. The Leesdale Local had two locomotive units, each with two exits. The engineer and conductor were in the lead unit; the brakeman occupied the second unit. After the collision, the second unit remained upright, and the brakeman was able to exit unassisted through the rear cab door. Because the lead unit came to rest on its left side, the door on the right side of the cab (behind the engineer's seat) was too high for the crewmembers to reach. The second door, through the nose of the unit, was blocked by the Metrolink locomotive.

As a result of the collision, a fire started that was fed by diesel fuel leaking from a fuel tank that had separated from the Metrolink locomotive. The leaking fuel tank had come to rest next to the occupied cab of the lead Leesdale Local locomotive. While efforts were underway to suppress the fire, firefighters heard pounding coming from the lead locomotive cab. They looked through the cab windows and saw that the two crewmembers were trapped inside. Firefighters attempted to break the windshield and cut a front window, but neither effort was successful. They were finally able to cut through the rubber molding around the window and remove it. Upon removing the window, they found that the cab was filled with smoke.

According to the captain in charge of fire suppression, one of the crewmembers exited the cab with severe back injuries. The captain helped him to the triage area. The second crewmember was not able to move and could not exit the cab without assistance. Two firefighters removed him from the cab and carried him to the triage area.

Metrolink Train 111. As firefighters set to work getting passengers out of the first passenger coach, which was the most seriously damaged car, additional deputies and officers from the California Highway Patrol began to arrive on scene. Firefighters working deeper into the car began handing debris to the deputies and officers, who then removed the debris from the car. As victims were removed from the wreckage, they were placed on backboards and carried from the car by a line of deputies and officers. This activity at the first passenger coach continued for 3 to 4 hours.

Meanwhile, teams were searching the second and third passenger coaches. A police officer said that when he entered the second passenger coach, he saw that most of the passengers had exited but that six people were still in the car and that they could not move. Three were on the first level, and three were on the second level. Firefighters from the Los Angeles County Fire Department next arrived at the second and third cars and began triaging the passengers. In the third passenger coach were four or five passengers who received assistance.

Survivors removed from all of the cars were first taken to a patient holding area on the north side of the train. As the patient numbers increased, they were moved to a patient collection area farther away from the train. Law enforcement officers helped carry the backboards and baskets used to move patients to the patient collection area. Chaplains began arriving on scene and assisted fire department personnel. A temporary morgue was established to the side of the wreckage.

Firefighters sent to walk the UP train to check the train's contents reported that they found nothing of concern. A UP representative told responders where to find a copy of the train consist, which the firefighters retrieved from the lead UP locomotive.

Fire department and railroad resources were coordinated through a city fire department rail liaison officer working with Metrolink personnel. Overnight, Metrolink's security coordinator was placed in charge of the railroad's response. Metrolink had staged heavy equipment about a half mile away from the accident site. A UP representative also coordinated in the arrival and staging of heavy equipment and equipment operators.

Battalion chiefs met periodically with representatives of the urban search and rescue teams and the railroads to plan operations. Rescue efforts continued until about 1:00 a.m. on September 13, at which time rescue operations transitioned to recovery operations. The Metrolink locomotive was pulled away from the first passenger car about 8:00 a.m. on September 13. Recovery operations continued until the final victim was recovered about 2:00 p.m. on September 13.

Injuries

Table 1. Injuries.

Injury Type	Train Crews	Passengers	Emergency Responders	Total
Fatal	1	24	0	25
Serious	3	25	0	28
Minor	1	71	1	73
None	0	0	0	0
Total	5	120	1	126
Title 49 CFR 840.2 defines fatality as the death of a person either at the time an accident occurs or within 24 hours thereafter. Title 49 CFR 830.2 defines serious injury as "an injury which: (1) requires hospitalization for more than 48 hours, commencing within 7 days from the date the injury was received; (2) results in a fracture of any bone (except simple fractures of fingers, toes or nose); (3) causes severe hemorrhages, nerve, or tendon damage; (4) involves any internal organ; or (5) involves second or third-degree burns, or any burn affecting more than 5 percent of the body surface."				

Damage

The Metrolink train 111 locomotive sustained substantial crush damage in the collision, with damage estimated as $3.5 million. The first passenger coach behind the locomotive was destroyed, at a cost of $2.2 million. The remaining two Metrolink passenger coaches were substantially damaged, with repair costs estimated as $1.5 million.

The UP estimated damages to the locomotives of the Leesdale Local as $1.2 million, with an additional $2.123 million in damages to cars and $200,000 losses in lading. Cleanup expenses were estimated as $500,000 for the UP and $670,000 for Metrolink. Damage to the track structure was estimated as $250,000. Total damages were estimated to be $12.143 million.

Personnel Information

Metrolink Train 111

The engineer and conductor of Metrolink train 111 at the time of the accident worked a regularly assigned 5-day week, Monday through Friday, with Saturdays and Sundays off. The crew had worked together on this assignment since April 15, 2008. The crew was scheduled to arrive at Moorpark at 4:45 p.m. They would then operate train 118 from Moorpark, departing at 4:57 p.m. and arriving at Union Station at 6:20 p.m. The crew would then operate train 119 from Union Station to Montalvo, departing at 6:40 p.m. and arriving at Montalvo at 8:35 p.m. They would go off duty at 9:05 p.m. with an average total time on duty of 10 hours 37 minutes.

Engineer. The engineer of Metrolink train 111, age 47, was hired by Connex Railroad, LLC,[18] (Connex) on June 25, 2005. Between November 1998 and June 2005, he had worked as an engineer for Amtrak. Connex files disclosed no record of any formal disciplinary action with regard to the engineer. The engineer's record did show that he had received five "Letters of Counseling" (considered informal discipline) in the previous 4 years. In December 2005, he was counseled about his failure to report for duty on his assigned job. In December 2006, he was counseled about his failure to report that his conductor was late for a job assignment. In August 2006 and again in December 2006, he was counseled about the number of times he had been absent from work during the previous 12 months, a number that constituted a violation of the Connex attendance policy. Two days before the accident, the engineer was counseled about his responsibility for delaying train 119 on August 19, 2008, at Moorpark station. As will be discussed in more detail later in this report, the engineer had, on two occasions, received oral counseling about his cell phone use while on duty.

The engineer's most recent recertification occurred on July 24, 2007 and was valid until September 10, 2010. Connex records disclosed that the engineer had successfully completed his last rules examination on May, 14, 2008. A check of the engineer's work history revealed his last missed workday was September 3, 2008, when he used an accrued personal day.

Time sheets provided by Connex showed that the engineer worked the same schedule for the four days, Monday through Thursday, preceding the day of the accident. Under that schedule, he went on duty at 5:54 a.m. at Montalvo. He departed on train 106 at 6:44 a.m. and arrived at Los Angeles Union Station at 8:28 a.m. He was off duty from 9:26 a.m. until returning to work at 2:00 p.m. He departed Union Station westbound on train 111 at 3:35 p.m. and arrived at Moorpark at 4:45 p.m. He departed Moorpark eastbound at 4:57 p.m. on train 118 and arrived at Union Station at 6:20 p.m. At 6:40 p.m., he departed Union Station on train 119 and arrived at Montalvo at 8:35 p.m. He went off duty at 9:05 p.m.

On the day of the accident, as on the previous 4 days, the engineer went on duty at 5:54 a.m. He operated a train from 6:44 a.m. until going off duty at 9:26 a.m. He returned to duty at

---

[18] Connex Railroad, LLC, under contract to the SCRRA, provided the locomotive engineers and conductors for Metrolink trains, along with the management, administrative, and training services required to support rail operations.

2:00 p.m. At 3:35 p.m., he departed on train 111. At the time of the accident, the engineer had most recently been on duty for the second portion of his workday for about 2 hours 22 minutes.

Conductor. The train 111 conductor, age 57, was hired by Connex on June 25, 2005. He was previously employed as a conductor by Amtrak beginning in March 1997. According to Connex records, the conductor had successfully completed his last operational rules tests on May 13, 2008. Connex files disclosed no record of any formal disciplinary action with regard to the conductor. The conductor received informal discipline in the form of a "Letter of Counseling" regarding his responsibility for the delay of train 119 on August 19, 2008, at Moorpark station.

The conductor said that he had worked on the Monday and Thursday before the accident and had been off on Tuesday and Wednesday. On each of his workdays, he awoke at 3:00 a.m. and left for work at 4:00 a.m. He departed on a train at 6:44 a.m. and worked until 9:26 a.m., when he went off duty. He worked the second part of his day from 2:00 p.m. until 9:05 p.m. He worked this same morning schedule on the day of the accident and was into the second portion of his workday when the accident occurred. At that time, he had been on duty for the second portion of his workday for about 2 hours 22 minutes, and awake for about 13 hours 22 minutes.

Union Pacific Leesdale Local

Three crewmembers (engineer, conductor, and brakeman) were on the Leesdale Local at the time of the accident. This was the regular assignment for the engineer and brakeman; the conductor was an extra-board[19] employee filling in for the regularly assigned conductor.

Engineer. The engineer, age 65, was hired by the UP railroad on April 3, 1969. UP files disclosed no record of any disciplinary action pertaining to the engineer in the 2 years prior to the accident. The engineer's most recent recertification occurred on September 3, 2008. It is valid until January 31, 2010.

The engineer stated that he arose every day between 6:00 a.m. and 6:30 a.m., departed his residence for work at 10:30 a.m., and went on duty at 11:30 a.m. He said he usually went off duty between 6:30 p.m. and 7:00 p.m.[20] He added he retired each evening no later than 11:30 p.m. At the time of the accident, he had been awake for approximately 10 hours and on duty for just under 5 hours.

Conductor. The conductor, age 32, was hired by the UP Railroad on June 22, 1998. UP files disclosed no record of any disciplinary action with regard to the conductor in the 2 years prior to the accident.

The conductor said that he awoke about 9:30 a.m. on Monday, September 8. He went on duty at 11:30 a.m. on the Leesdale Local, worked until about 6:30 p.m., and returned home. He

---

[19] The *extra board* is a list of qualified employees available to fill in for regularly assigned workers or to work non-scheduled assignments.

[20] According to UP records, with the exception of Tuesday, September 9, when he went off duty at 6:55 p.m., the engineer went on duty at 11:30 a m. and off duty at 6:30 p.m. each day beginning Monday, September 8, through the day of the accident.

said he retired for the evening between 11:00 p.m. and 11:30 p.m. He did not work the following day, Tuesday, September 9, and awoke about 10:00 a.m. He retired for the evening about 11:45 p.m. He did not work the following day, Wednesday, September 10, and arose about 8:45 a.m. He retired for the evening about 1:00 a.m. the following day, Thursday, September 11. He arose later that day about noon, again did not work, and retired for the evening about 11:00 p.m. He awoke the following morning, Friday, September 12 at 9:30 a.m. when he was called for duty. He reported for duty at 11:30 a.m. to work the Leesdale Local. At the time of the accident, he had been awake for about 6 hours 42 minutes and on duty for just under 5 hours.

Brakeman. The brakeman, age 64, was hired by the UP on January 2, 1965. UP files disclosed no record of any disciplinary action with regard to the brakeman in the 2 years prior to the accident.

The brakeman recalled that on Tuesday, September 9, and Wednesday, September 10, he arose about 7:00 a.m., reported for work by 11:30 a.m., and went off duty about 7:00 p.m. On both evenings, he retired by 9:30 p.m. He awoke at 6:00 a.m. on Thursday, September 11, reported for duty at 11:30 a.m., and went off duty about 7:00 p.m. He retired for the evening between 9:30 p.m. and 10:00 p.m. He awoke the following morning, Friday, September 12, at 6:00 a.m. and reported for duty at 11:30 a.m. At the time of the accident the brakeman had been awake for almost 10 hours 30 minutes and on duty for just under 5 hours.

Person A

The individual referred to in this report as Person A is a teenager and a self-described "rail fan."[21] He said he has several friends who were also rail fans (two of whom are referred to later in this report as "Person B" and "Person C") and that he met the accident engineer in May 2008 through one of those friends. He said he would occasionally see the engineer at various rail stations while he was watching trains and that the two would sometimes engage in brief conversations centered around rail operations or the engineer's career. The conversations were brief, he said, "because [the engineer] would usually be driving the train, and he'd come in, you know, say 'Hi,' and leave."

Person A said that he would occasionally send text messages to the engineer while he was on duty and that the engineer would respond "when he got a chance." Person A recalled having spoken to the engineer via cell phone about 12:30 p.m. on the day of the accident. He said the engineer sounded "happy and cheerful, like I always remembered him to be." He also remembered that they exchanged a "few" text messages that morning, "because that was a very busy shift for him."

Person A recalled that after 3:35 p.m. on the afternoon of the accident, he received a text message from the engineer about every 15 minutes. He said he sent the engineer a text message shortly after 4:00 p.m. and received the last text message response from him at 4:22 p.m. He recalled the message pertained to an Amtrak train that was running behind schedule.

---

[21] A *rail fan* is an individual for whom railroading is a hobby. Rail fans may focus their interest on one or several aspects of railroading, such as railroad history, locomotives, rolling stock, or overall train operations.

Person A said he was at home after receiving the text message at 4:22 p.m. and that he had turned on the news sometime after that time and learned of the accident. He said that when he heard that the accident had occurred at Chatsworth, he immediately knew it was the engineer's train, as it was the only Metrolink train that would have been there at that time.

Train and Mechanical Information

Metrolink Train 111

Metrolink train 111 consisted of one diesel-electric locomotive unit, two passenger coach cars, and one passenger coach/cab control car. The locomotive was about 58 feet long, and each of the cars was 85 feet long, for a total train length of 313 feet.

The first two passenger cars of the train were conventional coaches manufactured by Bombardier Transportation Corporation (Bombardier) and delivered in the 2001-2002 time frame. The remaining passenger coach was, at the time of the accident, operating as a conventional passenger coach although it was also a cab control car with an operating compartment from which the train was run when operating in the "push" mode (locomotive at the rear). (See figure 5.) The cab control car was manufactured by the Urban Transportation Development Corporation (UTDC) (now a part of Bombardier) and delivered in December 1992. Both passenger coaches and the coach/cab control car are referred to as BiLevel coaches.

Figure 5. Bombardier BiLevel passenger coach of the type involved in this accident

The coach bodies were a semi-monocoque[22] construction that incorporates a non-linear structural steel center sill element manufactured from a low-alloy high-tensile steel and an aluminum alloy superstructure. Structural test reports indicates a delivery requirement that the carbody structure resist a minimum static end (compressive) load of 800,000 pounds, as applied on the centerline of draft, without any permanent deformation to any member of the car structure. Collision posts are provided in the front bulkhead to help prevent carbody telescoping.[23] Delivery documentation indicated that static end-load structural testing was successfully conducted on an exemplar railcar representing each delivery series of cars involved in this accident. The test results showed that the car structural design has been demonstrated to satisfy the requirements of the Association of American Railroad's Manual of Standards and Practices and of 49 *Code of Federal Regulations* (CFR) 229.141(a), both of which include a test requirement that the carbody structure resist a minimum static end (compressive) load of 800,000 pounds.

Although referred to as "bi-level" or "double-deck," these coaches actually have three separate levels of passenger seating accommodations. The design incorporates two full decks (an upper and lower) in the center of the railcar, with an intermediate-level deck situated over the truck assemblies at each end of the car. All three decks provide passenger seating. The BiLevel coaches are all configured to the same basic passenger seating arrangement. The only significant difference between a conventional coach and a cab control car is that the latter is equipped with an operator's cab compartment at its leading end. The cab control car can accommodate 142 passengers; the conventional coach seats 143. Both coach designs have a crush load[24] capacity of about 360 passengers.

Two stairwells in each coach[25] provide access between the lower-level deck, the intermediate level at each opposite end of the railcar, and the upper-level deck. Passengers enter and exit the coaches through four main pneumatically operated pocket door sets[26] on the lower-level deck of each railcar, with two sets of doors on each side. A vestibule area is provided between the main side-exit doors at each end of the lower-level deck. An emergency release handle adjacent to each main side-exit door may be used to release one of the sliding pocket door panels at each door location. A restroom is at one end of the lower-level deck. A door at each end bulkhead on the intermediate level provides passage to adjacent railcars.

---

[22] In *monocoque* construction, the structural load is borne by the vehicle's external skin rather than by an internal frame. In *semi-monocoque* construction, internal bracing is added to supplement the load-bearing capability of the vehicle skin.

[23] *Telescoping* occurs when a railcar body breaches the end-structure of another carbody and passes into the structure of that carbody, emulating a "telescoping" action. Telescoping can also occur when a single carbody is placed under severe compressive axial loading that causes a localized structural failure with consequent partial overlapping of the carbody sidewall panels.

[24] The *crush load* is the maximum number of passengers that can possibly be riding in the railcar (standing and sitting).

[25] The stairwells are located approximately 1/4 of the car length from each end of the car.

[26] A *pocket door* is a door that opens by sliding horizontally into a narrow compartment within the wall adjacent to the doorway.

Passenger seating accommodations on board the Metrolink BiLevel railcars consist of a combination of transverse and longitudinal-mounted fixed seat assemblies,[27] with the seat assemblies installed on both sides of a longitudinally oriented center aisle passageway on all three deck levels. Almost all of the transverse mounted fixed seat assemblies in the Metrolink BiLevel coach railcar fleet are arranged in a "2+2," paired/side-by-side configuration (also referred to as a "paired seating sets" arrangement). Many of the paired seating sets are arranged in an opposing face-to-face layout with the balance of the paired seating sets arranged so that the paired seating sets are all facing in the same direction.

Each Metrolink BiLevel railcar is equipped with eight workstation tables, four on the upper level and two at each end of the intermediate level. These tables are fitted between paired seating sets of opposing passenger seats. The tables are a basic design consisting of a one-piece tabletop assembly that is cantilevered from the carbody sidewall and supported by a single pedestal leg. The tabletops are trapezoidal in shape, approximately of a uniform size, and manufactured of a high-pressure laminate without any form of safety padding.

Inspections and Maintenance. An examination of inspection and maintenance history records for each of the Metrolink cars and the locomotive unit involved in the accident revealed that the equipment had received all required inspections and scheduled maintenance.

Postaccident Inspections. Investigators inspected the rear two Metrolink cars at the accident site and tested the air brake system.[28] The air brake system on the cars was charged to 111 pounds per square inch (psi), then a 20-psi reduction was made and a leakage test conducted. The cars had 2-psi-per-minute brake pipe leakage.[29] The air pressure reduction caused all the train tread and disc brakes to apply as designed. All the contact surfaces were smooth and work-polished.

The brake pipe was recharged (pressurized), and the brake shoes released. An emergency application (a rapid reduction of brake pipe pressure to 0 psi) was then initiated from the locomotive unit. The brakes at each location again applied; however, the disc brake at one location on the cab control car subsequently released. The actuator at that location was found to be loose and moved more than normal when shaken by hand.

The air brake systems on the Metrolink locomotive unit and first car were damaged in the accident to the extent that no meaningful test could be performed. The contact surfaces of both were inspected and found to be smooth and work-polished. The front truck on the locomotive unit had thermal cracking at several sites around the circumference of the wheels.

---

[27] A *fixed seat* is a passenger seat that is permanently configured in a given location such that it cannot otherwise be readily reconfigured (by operational or maintenance personnel) to face any other direction.

[28] Train brakes are activated using air pressure maintained in the "brake pipe," a continuous pipe extending from the locomotives to the last car in a train when all cars and their air hoses are coupled. (The term "brake pipe" is also used when referring to a single car.) A reduction in brake pipe pressure causes the brake shoes on each car to apply, with the degree of application proportional to the amount of the pressure reduction. When the reduction is stopped and brake pipe pressure increases, the brakes release.

[29] Federal Railroad Administration regulations (49 *Code of Federal Regulations* 238.313) allow up to 5-psi-per-minute leakage so long as such leakage does not affect service performance.

Event Recorders. The Metrolink locomotive unit was equipped with an event recorder that sustained significant thermal and crush damage in the accident. The damaged recorder was recovered and sent to the NTSB's Vehicle Recorders Laboratory in Washington, D.C., where investigators removed its memory module. On September 18, 2008, an NTSB investigator took the module to the recorder's manufacturer, Bach-Simpson, where the recorded data were successfully downloaded. The Metrolink cab control car (the last car of the train in this accident) also had an event recorder. This recorder was undamaged in the accident, and investigators downloaded its data on scene.

Leesdale Local

The UP Leesdale Local consisted of two diesel-electric locomotive units and 17 cars (7 loads and 10 empties). The train, including the locomotive units, weighed 1,523 tons and was 1,164 feet long.

Postaccident Inspections. The rear seven cars from the Leesdale Local were inspected at Moorpark, California, on Sunday, September 14, 2008. The air brake system on the cars was charged to 90 pounds per square inch, gauge, (psig), then a 20-psi reduction was made and a leakage test conducted. The cars had 1/2-psi-per-minute brake pipe leakage, which was within Federal allowable limits. When the brake pipe pressure was reduced, the brakes applied at each location, as expected. When the brake system was recharged, all the brake shoes released normally except for those at one location where a new wheel was evident.

Event Recorders. The Leesdale Local had event recorders on both locomotive units. Data from the event recorder on the second unit was downloaded at the scene. Data from the recorder on the lead unit could not be downloaded on scene;[30] therefore the recorder was sent to the NTSB's Vehicle Recorders Laboratory in Washington, D.C. On September 28, 2008, with the assistance of the locomotive's manufacturer, data from the lead unit event recorder were successfully downloaded.

Video Recorders. The Leesdale Local locomotives were also equipped with Wabtec/March Networks VideoTrax digital video recording device. These devices record audio, video, and some parametric data. The video cameras were mounted to provide a forward-facing view through the locomotive window. Black-and-white 720 x 480-pixel images are stored at a rate of 15 per second. A microphone captures sound from outside the locomotive cab. GPS time/date, position, and speed are captured along with horn and pneumatic control switch status (on or off). The recorders can store approximately 80 hours of video/audio/data on a 60 Gb removable hard disk. The video cameras on both locomotive units were sent to the UP playback station in Omaha, Nebraska, where an NTSB investigator coordinated retrieval of the information.

---

[30] Locomotive event recorder data are typically downloaded while the recorder is installed in the locomotive and the unit is running. Damage to the lead unit of the Leesdale Local prevented this method of data retrieval.

Wreckage

Because of the urgent need to conduct rescue operations for passengers of the Metrolink train, the accident site was significantly disturbed before NTSB investigators arrived on the scene. During the rescue and recovery efforts, some of the derailed railroad equipment was moved a short distance from where it initially came to rest and was available for examination. Investigators used map graphics (based on aerial photographs) as well as aerial and ground-based photographs to document the condition and location of this equipment before it was relocated. For the railroad equipment that had not been disturbed or relocated, investigators were able to examine and record observations of the physical aspects of the accident scene. The information in the remainder of this section is based on this combination of documentation and direct examination.

Metrolink Train 111

The three Metrolink passenger coaches remained where they initially came to rest, although certain components of the lead passenger coach had been disturbed during the efforts to extricate passengers. For example, much of the carbody side and roof panels and many of the interior components (seats, floor, partitions, hand-hold stanchion posts) had been placed temporarily in a debris pile immediately adjacent to where the railcar initially came to rest.

The other derailed railroad equipment, which included the Metrolink locomotive and almost all of the UP equipment, had been moved but remained available for subsequent post-recovery examination.

Locomotive. The Metrolink locomotive, which had been operating in a cab-forward orientation, came to rest on its right side (relative to its normal direction of travel) with the locomotive carbody longitudinally oriented roughly parallel to the track centerline. Obvious severe collision impact damage was evident on the front end, both side panel areas, the operator's cab, and aft end of the locomotive. The locomotive's front end was firmly wedged against the front end of the lead UP locomotive, and its aft end penetrated the leading bulkhead panel of the passenger coach to which it was coupled. The rear portion of the locomotive came to rest within the confines of the occupant compartment of that first passenger car. In this position, the locomotive carbody occupied approximately 52 feet, or approximately the forward two-thirds, of the passenger coach. (See figure 6.)

Figure 6. The force of the collision drove the Metrolink locomotive about 52 feet into the passenger space of the first coach behind the locomotive.

The operator's cab, which had been occupied solely by the train engineer, sustained a complete loss of survivable space. Post-recovery measurements of the locomotive indicated that the front and rear ends of the unit had been compressively displaced by about 15 feet and about 1 foot, respectively. The locomotive had thus, as a result of the collision, compressed from its original 58-foot length to a length of about 42 feet.

The fuel tank separated from the locomotive and was found resting on the track ballast a short distance to the right side of the track, approximately adjacent to where the front of the locomotive came to rest. The tank was breached and lost some of its contents of diesel fuel, which burned in a fire.

The lead power-truck assembly had separated from the locomotive and was found resting upright, close to the centerline of the track approximately adjacent to the mid-point of where the lead UP locomotive had come to rest. The aft power-truck assembly remained attached to the locomotive.

First Passenger Coach. The first passenger coach aft of the locomotive sustained severe structural damage that compromised its occupant survivable space. According to the on-scene emergency responders and representatives of the Los Angeles County coroner department, of the 24 passengers that were fatally injured in the accident, 22 were in this coach at the time of the collision. One fatally injured passenger was determined to have been in the second passenger coach, and the location of the other fatally injured passenger at the time of the collision could not be determined. The car showed no evidence of fire damage.

As a result of the collision, the passenger coach derailed and came to rest at the immediate right side of the track leaning severely toward its right side. Because of the penetration of the aft end of the locomotive through the leading bulkhead panel, the forward one-quarter of the coach (encompassing the intermediate-level passenger compartment, which is above the lead-end truck) separated at the center sill and telescoped into the carbody, along with the lead truck, which remained attached to this section of the car. The telescoping action purged the entire interior carbody content in the forward two-thirds of the car such that only the outer sidewalls, which had bulged and peeled outward, and roof structure of the carbody shell remained. Within this area, the leading-end intermediate-, the lower-, and the upper-level passenger compartments sustained a complete loss of occupant survivable space. The aft intermediate-level passenger compartment (located above the aft-end truck), including the spaces of the aft stairwells, were generally undamaged.

The aft truck assembly had separated from the car and was found resting upright on the track ballast immediately adjacent to its normal location on the car frame.

The coupler shank at the aft end of the car was fractured and bent downward. The coupler head had separated from the shank, which caused this car to separate from the second passenger coach. The separation distance between the two cars was about 32 feet.

Second Passenger Coach. The second passenger coach from the locomotive did not sustain severe structural damage in the accident, nor was its occupant survival space significantly compromised. Only one of the fatally injured passengers was identified as having been occupying this car at the time of the collision.

Investigators were able to examine this car before it was moved from its original postaccident position. The car did not derail and came to rest in its normal orientation on the track. The car showed some interior damage and several ripples along the exterior carbody, but it exhibited no obvious exterior or interior catastrophic collision impact damage. The interior damage consisted primarily of fractured seatbacks, dislodged seats, bent and separated stanchion (vertical handhold) posts, dislodged or separated slider door and utility compartment panels, dislodged or separated work-station tables, and dislodged or separated ceiling panels. The car showed no evidence of fire damage.

A number of emergency windows had been removed by emergency responders. The coupler shank at the leading end was fractured and bent upward, and the coupler head still engaged the aft coupler head of the first passenger coach. At its aft end, the car remained coupled to the third passenger coach.

Third Passenger Coach. The third passenger coach, although equipped as a cab control car, was operating as a conventional coach at the time of the accident. Investigators were able to examine this car before it was moved from its original postaccident position. The car did not sustain severe structural damage during the collision, nor was its occupant survival space significantly compromised. The car showed no evidence of fire damage.

The car, which had been operating B-end forward, did not derail and came to rest in its normal orientation on the track. The car showed no evidence of exterior or interior catastrophic collision impact damage. The interior damage was similar to that exhibited by the second passenger coach, including emergency windows that had been removed during the response.

UP Leesdale Local

Lead Locomotive. Damage to the lead locomotive of the UP train consisted primarily of extensive frontal damage and some fire damage. No loss of occupant survival space in the locomotive cab occurred.

Trailing Locomotive. The trailing locomotive had been disturbed from its immediate postaccident condition and relocated. As a result, no detailed assessment could be made of the damage the unit sustained during the collision. According to UP officials who were on the scene immediately after the accident, damage to the unit consisted primarily of substantial distortion to the roof of the operator's cab. A segment of the roof panel had apparently been struck by a derailed freight car during the collision.

Topanga Switch

Investigators examined the power switch machine at CP Topanga and found the switch points split in mid-stroke, indicating that the switch had been run through in the trailing position.[31] (See figure 7.) Additional visual inspection revealed that the throw-rod, basket rod, and switch machine internal throw-rod were bent and damaged. Because of the nature and extent of the damage, Metrolink signal personnel had to replace the switch machine.

Meteorological Information

The Van Nuys surface weather station, about 6.2 miles east of Chatsworth, reported weather conditions at 3:51 p.m. on September 12, 2008, as follows: daylight, clear skies, haze, calm winds, and a temperature of 73° F with visibility of 4 miles.

Track Information

The main track preceding CP Topanga generally consists of 136-pound continuous welded rail.[32] The rail is seated in 16 by 7 3/4-inch double shoulder tie plates that lie between the

---

[31] *Switch points* are the movable, tapered rail sections that are moved either against or away from the stationary (stock) rail to allow a train to continue straight through the switch or to be diverted by the switch onto another track. Trains approaching the switch from the side with the tapered switch points are said to be making a "facing point" movement. Trains approaching from the opposite direction are making a "trailing point" movement.

[32] *Continuous welded rail* (CWR) consists of rail sections that have been welded together in lengths greater than 400 feet.

bottom surface of the rail and the top surface of timber crossties. The rail is fastened through the tie plates to standard timber crossties with four lag screws, two on the gauge side (between the rails) and two on the field side (outside the rails). A 6° curve begins just west of the Topanga switch. Beginning at this point, the crosstie type changes from wood to concrete.

Figure 7. CP Topanga switch looking east, in the direction the Leesdale Local was traveling. Circles highlight damage to switch points and components consistent with the switch having been run through in a trailing point movement by the Metrolink train traveling in the opposite direction.

In the wooden crosstie section, the ties are predominantly box anchored (four rail anchors per crosstie, two rail anchors applied to each rail, a rail anchor on each side of a crosstie) with rail anchors applied to every crosstie. The rail in the concrete tie sections is anchored on every tie with two elastic fasteners. Both areas of track are supported by a mixture of semi-angular granite ballast that fills the crosstie cribs. The depth of the ballast was estimated at 20 to 22 inches. The ballast shoulders measured 20 inches wide on tangent (straight track) and 24 inches wide in the curve. Investigators did not observe any fouled ballast conditions.

The Topanga switch itself is constructed of continuous welded rail, with the switch point area completely welded (without rail joints). The switch uses Samson switch points and stock rails that are beveled for a protected fit of the switch point against the stock rail.

Leading up to CP Topanga westbound, the maximum authorized speed is 70 mph for passenger trains, which requires that the track be maintained to Federal Railroad Administration (FRA) class 4 standards. Between CP Topanga and tunnel 28, a permanent speed restriction of 40 mph is in effect because of the 6° curvature in the track. Because of the lower maximum speed, this track is maintained to FRA class 3 standards.

Signal Information

General

Control points on the Ventura Subdivision between CP Davis and CP Bernson are equipped with Vital Harmon Logic Controller processors, and intermediate signals are equipped with Electro-Code 4 processors, both of which are provided by General Electric Transportation Services.

The Metrolink centralized traffic control system between CP Davis and CP Bernson uses Safetran V-20 Colorlight signals and GRS Sentinel signals. The system uses US&S M-23A low-voltage power-operated switch machines. Signal track circuits are controlled by Electro Code 4 electronic coded track circuits between control points and d.c. track circuits within control point sections. Signals are arranged for movement in either direction.

Until the dispatcher has selected and cleared a route for a train, or trains, the signals at either side of a control point are set to display a red aspect. Once the dispatcher has requested a route that is not precluded by existing train traffic, the signals governing that route change to display the appropriate aspects.

The Metrolink Operations Center uses the Digicon computerized dispatching system to align routes for train movements. To facilitate traffic flow, dispatchers will often plan a sequence of train movements in advance and then "stack" requests for those routes in the Digicon system. The Digicon system will place those stacked requests in a queue and carry them out, in the order in which they were entered, as train movements allow. For example, on the day of the accident, the dispatcher selected the first route, which called for the eastbound Leesdale Local to proceed from CP Davis along the main track and through the siding at CP Topanga. Before this move could be completed, the dispatcher requested a second routing, which would allow train 111 to proceed westbound on the main track through the switch at CP Topanga. Because the first route the dispatcher had selected (for the Leesdale Local) took precedence, the request regarding train 111 was placed in the queue within the Digicon system. The Digicon system was designed to carry out this request—which involved realigning the Topanga switch for the main line and displaying a *clear* indication on the westbound Topanga signal—only after the Leesdale Local was in the siding and clear of the main track. Until then, the design of the Digicon system prevented it from transmitting the dispatcher's route commands for train 111 to the appropriate Harmon Vital Logic Controllers in the field. The logic circuits within the controllers are also designed not to allow conflicting or opposing routes. That is, once the switches are set for an eastbound train to move into the siding, the system will not (because of the interrupted electrical circuit caused by the movement of the switch) allow the westbound signal at CP Topanga to show any aspect other than red.

Some of the signals on the Ventura Subdivision, including the signals at CP Topanga, are "approach lit," meaning that they will display a signal aspect only when a train enters the segment of track governed by that signal. At other times, the signals are in the "conservation" mode and remain dark as a way of reducing maintenance and extending the life of the signal lamps. Thus, even though the signal circuitry of the westbound CP Topanga signal called for a *stop* indication at the time of the accident, the red aspect of the signal did not actually illuminate until train 111 passed intermediate signal 4451, just east of the Chatsworth station, at 4:18:41 p.m.

Review of Recorded Signal Data

Downloaded data from Digicon event logs at the Metrolink dispatching center and signal event recorders in the field indicate that, at the time of the accident, the westbound signal at CP Topanga was displaying a red aspect (*stop* indication) and the dispatcher's stacked request to clear this signal was waiting in the queue in the Digicon dispatching system.

The data logs for each signal reflect the aspect being displayed at any given time by a notation in the log indicating which (if any) repeater relays for the various aspects are energized. Because the current to energize the relay coil must pass through the lamp (light bulb) of the aspect, the relay can only be energized (which moves the relay armature to the "up" position) if the lamp for that aspect is intact and that current is flowing through it. If the lamp is not energized, or if the bulb is burned out, the armature of the repeater relay for that aspect will be in the "down" position. Signal event recorder logs for the westbound Topanga signal showed that as train 111 approached the westbound Topanga signal, the armature of the repeater relay for the red aspect was in the "up" position, indicating that the aspect was energized; the relays for the yellow and green aspects were down and therefore not energized.

Operations Information

General

The SCRRA is the joint powers authority that oversees the Southern California commuter rail service known as Metrolink. The system comprises 7 rail routes, 56 stations, and 512 total route miles of track in six counties. Metrolink owns 37 locomotives and 135 commuter coaches and leases additional coaches. The system transports about 45,000 passengers each day.

The accident occurred at milepost 444.12[33] on Metrolink's Ventura Subdivision, about 33 miles west of Los Angeles. Timetable direction is east–west. This part of the subdivision features a single main track. All train movements are governed by wayside signal indications of a traffic control system administered from Metrolink's operations center in Pomona, California. A dispatcher at the operations center directly controls switches and signals at control points. (See

---

[33] Milepost numbers decrease from east to west.

figure 8.) Between control points, intermediate signals automatically display the signal indications appropriate for the existing track and traffic conditions.

Trains operate in both directions on the single track main line, with the subdivision averaging 6 freight trains, 18 Metrolink trains, and 12 Amtrak trains daily. Maximum speeds are 60 mph for freight trains and 79 mph for passenger trains. Because of the curvature of the track in the area of the accident, maximum allowable speed (between mileposts 442.6 and 444.5) is 40 mph.

Figure 8. Westbound signal at CP Topanga displaying a red aspect (indicating stop.)

Transportation services and operating crews are provided by transportation contractor Connex.[34] On June 25, 2005, Connex entered into a 5-year contract with SCRRA to provide Metrolink with operating crews, management personnel, and training support. These services had previously been provided by Amtrak.

---

[34] Connex Railroad, LLC, is a unit of Veolia Transportation, Inc., which entered the U.S. transportation market in 2001.

Operating Rules and Efficiency Testing

Train operations on the Metrolink system are governed by the *General Code of Operating Rules*, 5th edition, effective April 13, 2005, and by timetable and special instructions, supplemented by Metrolink's *Manual of Instructions* effective 12:01 a.m. on September 1, 2007.

Each railroad, under Title 49 CFR Part 217, "Railroad Operating Rules," must carry out a program of operational tests and inspections (efficiency tests) of operating crewmembers. The Metrolink efficiency testing program, administered by Connex, became effective on June 26, 2005. The program was revised on July 1, 2008.

Under the program, tests were to be spread out and not confined to specific times and days of the month. The tests were to include Metrolink and foreign line crews operating over SCRRA property. At least half of the tests were to be on operating rules and special instructions. Testing methods included visual observation, monitoring of live and previously recorded radio and telephone transmissions, scrutiny of locomotive event recorder data, and use of radar or other approved wayside speed monitoring devices.

Medical and Toxicological Information

A review of the Metrolink engineer's railroad medical records showed that he had been diagnosed with type 2 diabetes and was being treated with multiple medications, including less-than-maximum doses of metformin, glipizide, and pioglitazone. The engineer also had high blood pressure, which records showed was being effectively controlled by use of the prescription medication benazepril. The engineer had been diagnosed HIV (Human Immunodeficiency Virus) positive about 2 years before the accident. He was being treated with anti-retroviral medications, which he was noted to be tolerating "very well with no side effects." These HIV diagnosis and retroviral medications had not been reported to the railroad medical department. Laboratory evaluation dated September 3, 2008 noted that the virus was not detected in the engineer's blood.

On July 6, 2007, an "Authorization to Work with Medication(s) and Without Work Restrictions" completed by the engineer's endocrinologist noted that the engineer was "fit for duty and can complete all duties of the position." The HIV diagnosis and antiretroviral medications were not noted on this form.

One month before the accident, the engineer's weight was recorded as 254 pounds. His height was recorded as 6 feet during a company physical examination in 2005. In December 2004, records of a physician visit noted that the engineer "may have sleep apnea, but he has no way of knowing. He thinks he does snore a lot ...." The autopsy report on the engineer noted that his heart weighed 430 grams and that "All chambers are dilated."

Pursuant to 49 *Code of Federal Regulations* (CFR) 219, Subpart C, "Post-Accident Toxicological Testing," toxicological specimens were obtained from the engineer and conductor of the Metrolink train and from the engineer, conductor, and brakeman of the Leesdale Local. The specimens were screened for cannabinoids, cocaine, opiates, amphetamines, methamphetamines, phencyclidine, barbiturates, benzodiazepines, and ethyl alcohol. Tests results for the Metrolink engineer and conductor and the Leesdale Local engineer and brakeman were negative for alcohol and the aforementioned drugs. The Leesdale Local conductor tested positive for cannabinoids (marijuana) in both blood and urine and negative for alcohol.[35] Test documentation indicated that the conductor's blood and urine specimens had been taken at 1:30 a.m. on September 13, 2008, the morning after the accident.

Remaining portions of the specimens obtained from the Metrolink engineer and conductor were sent to the Civil Aerospace Medical Institute (CAMI) in Oklahoma City, Oklahoma, for independent and broader toxicological analyses. In those tests, the Metrolink engineer tested positive for benazepril[36] and pioglitazone[37] in the blood and urine. The Metrolink conductor tested positive for fluoxetine[38] and norfluoxetine[39] in the blood and urine and for morphine (which had been administered during postaccident medical treatment) in the urine. The conductor's most recent physical examination had taken place in January 2006. At that time, the conductor had reported using fluoxetine, and his medical examination report had been reviewed and approved by the appropriate Connex authorities.

Asked about his positive test results, the Leesdale Local conductor stated that he had smoked marijuana "three times at most" in July and August 2008, saying that those occasions were his first use ever. He said he had not used marijuana on the day of, or several days before, the accident.

Metrolink Engineer's Use of a Wireless Device

Based on Verizon Wireless records, at the time of the accident, the Metrolink train engineer was in possession of an LG Model VX10000 "Voyager" wireless device (figure 9).[40] Among its features, the device is capable of browsing the Web, sending and receiving e-mail and text messages, downloading and playing music and video files, and capturing still images or video.

As part of this investigation, the NTSB obtained Verizon Wireless records for the Metrolink engineer's account covering the day of the accident as well as the previous 28 days. These records included the time and date of incoming and outgoing telephone calls as well as the time and date of any text messages sent or received, picture/video messages sent or received, and use of the device's Web browser.

The records indicate that between 6:05 a.m. and 4:22 p.m. on the day of the accident, the engineer sent or received a total of 95 text messages. During the time he was responsible for

---

[35] Results indicated the blood specimen contained 13.7 nanograms per milliliter (ng/ml) of carboxy-THC (the metabolite of the active ingredient of marijuana), tetrahydrocannabinol (THC), and 1.1 ng/ml of THC. The urine specimen contained 117 ng/ml of carboxy-THC.

[36] Benazepril is a prescription medication used to treat high blood pressure.

[37] Pioglitazone is a prescription medication used to treat type 2 diabetes.

[38] Fluoxetine (trade name Prozac) is a prescription medication used to treat depression, obsessive-compulsive disorder, some eating disorders, and panic attacks.

[39] Norfluoxetine is a metabolite of fluoxetine.

[40] Investigators were not able to locate the engineer's wireless device after the accident.

operation of a train (morning and afternoon shifts), the engineer sent 21 text messages, received 21 text messages, and made four outgoing telephone calls. The records show no picture message activity on the day of the accident, and Verizon representatives told investigators that their records showed no Web activity or use of "data services" by the engineer's wireless device on the day of the accident.[41]

Figure 9. LG wireless device Model VX10000 similar to the device used by the Metrolink engineer on the day of the accident. (Internet photograph)

The engineer began his morning shift on the day of the accident by moving train 106 out of the Montalvo station storage yard at 6:25 a.m. He operated the train in revenue service from 6:44 a.m. until arriving at Los Angeles Union Station at 8:25 a.m. He then operated in non-revenue service from Union Station to the central maintenance facility, arriving at 8:53 a.m. During these times, he sent 15 text messages, received 15 text messages, and made two phone calls (one lasting for 2 minutes 29 seconds, the other for 8 seconds). On the afternoon of the accident, as previously noted, the engineer sent six text messages and received seven during the time he was responsible for operating a train.

Pattern of Wireless Device Use

Investigators acquired the engineer's daily time tickets for the week before the accident and compared them with his cell phone records to determine whether the messaging activity on

---

[41] Because the device was not recovered, the contents of its internal memory could not be accessed.

the day of the accident was out of the ordinary for this individual. The results of that comparison are shown in figure 10.[42]

Records covering the 28 days before the accident showed 5 days with no text messaging and 4 days with more than 100 text messages sent or received in a 24-hour period. Activity on the remaining 19 days averaged about 40 messages per day.

The records also reflected the engineer's use of a wireless device to make voice calls while on duty. Figure 11 shows the telephone calls the engineer made or received (except for any that may have gone to voice mail) on the day of the accident and the preceding 7 days.

The *General Code of Operating Rules*[43] addresses the use of wireless or other electronic devices by train crewmembers as follows:

Rule 1.10 Games, Reading, or Electronic Devices

Unless permitted by the railroad, employees on duty must not:

- Play games.

- Read magazines, newspapers, or other literature not related to their duties.

- Use electronic devices not related to their duties.

Metrolink Timetable No. 5 *Additions and revisions to General Code of Operating Rules* dated July 8, 2008, adds to Rule 1.10:

[Unless permitted by the railroad, employees on duty must not:]

- Use cellular telephones when operating the controls of moving equipment except in emergencies.

Connex Metrolink Notice No. 17.08, on July 8, 2008, added the following to the previous version of the notice:

Electronic Devices:

The inappropriate use of electronic devices by employees on duty has been shown to be a contributing factor in personal injuries and rule violations. While you are working you are obligated to be completely focused on your job and the safe transportation of passengers. As a result, under most circumstances employees are prohibited from having personal electronic devices turned on and/or in their immediate vicinity while working.

---

[42] The times of train operation shown on the graph were taken from the engineer's time tickets, but these times may differ somewhat from the actual times that the engineer was responsible for operating a train.

[43] These rules apply equally to all railroads operating over SCRRA tracks.

Here are some examples of when company or personal cellular phones must not be used:

- While on the ground lining switches, meeting trains, standing next to main tracks or when performing other duties that require your undivided attention to safety and rules compliance

- While in the control compartment of a moving train

- To conduct non-railroad business while on or near trains

- Here are some examples of when company or personal cellular phones may be used:

- While in a layover facility

- When communicating railroad business on a stopped train such as troubleshooting mechanical problems or reporting information relating to an incident as the incident commander

- When in a crew transportation van

- Conductors reporting information to dispatchers relating to delays, etc., as long as the Conductor is not in the control compartment of a moving train

- Remember, when the train is moving or you are on the ground performing railroad business your personal electronic devices must be turned off and must not be within your reach-for example on the control stand or on your person. Personal electronic devices may be carried in your grip[44] if they are turned off. Conductors must have their company cellular phones "on" at all times while on duty.

Metrolink conductors (who have overall responsibility for the train except for its mechanical aspects and train handling) are issued a company cell phone to facilitate their communication with dispatchers. Train 111's conductor told investigators that he was allowed to use the cell phone for company business when actually on board the train. On the day of the accident, he used his company-provided cell phone to report the collision.

The Metrolink conductor said that about a month before the accident, in early August 2008, he observed the accident engineer using his cell phone while he (the engineer) was in the control compartment of a train preparing to leave the Moorpark station. He said he spoke to the engineer about it and the engineer, responding that he had been conducting union business, acknowledged that he needed to put the device away. The conductor said he later brought the incident to the attention of a supervisor but that he never heard back from the supervisor about

---

[44] *Grip* refers to the bag of personal belongings most crewmembers carry to and from work assignments.

any action that had been taken with regard to the inappropriate cell phone use. He also said he believed this to be an isolated event.

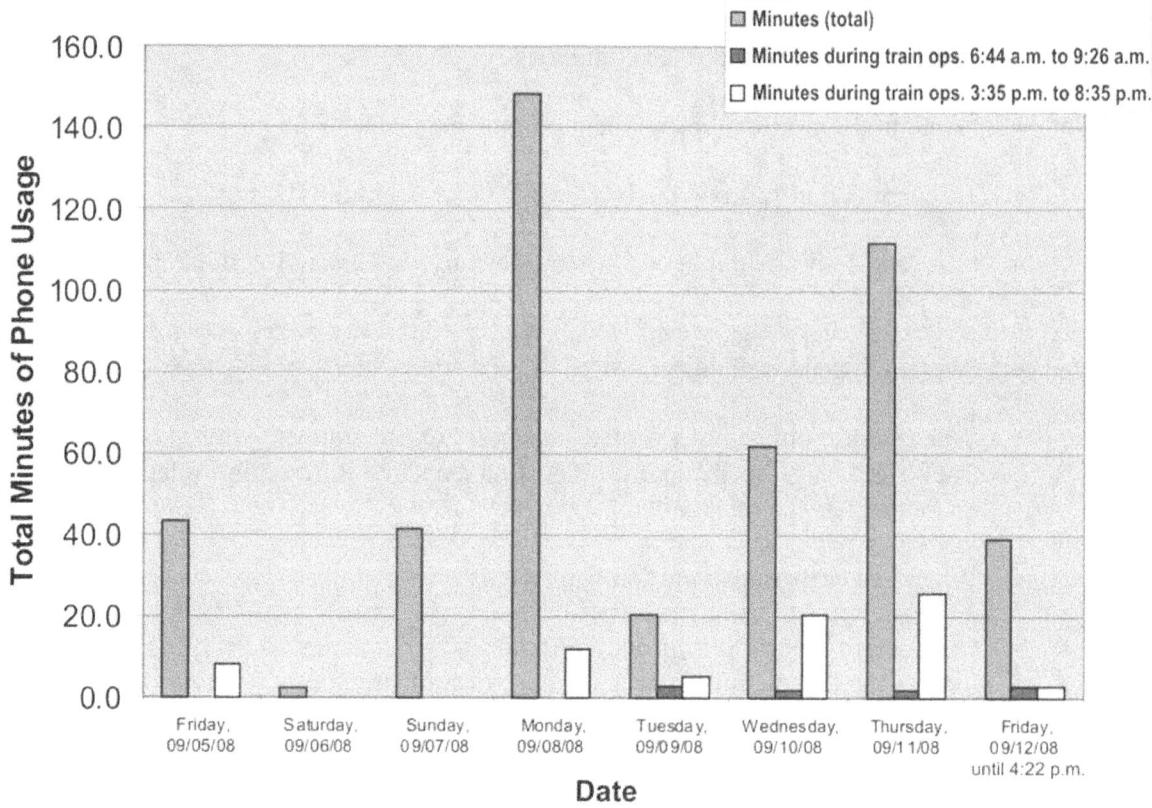

Figure 10. Text messages sent and received by the Metrolink engineer on the day of the accident and on the previous 7 days. (The engineer did not work Saturday or Sunday.)

At the March 3 and 4, 2009, public hearing on this accident held at NTSB headquarters in Washington, D.C., the Metrolink (Connex) manager of safety and operating practices recalled that he was the one to whom the conductor had reported the engineer's cell phone use. He said he immediately followed up with the engineer, briefing him not only on *General Code* Rule 1.10, but also on Connex's cell phone policy:

> During my conversation with him, I asked him where his phone was. He said it was stored away in his grip, that it was off. We talked about the cell phone policy. Confident that he understood the policy…, I did a couple observations within the next 2 weeks, and that was the last of any conversations or observations with the engineer [with regard to use of wireless devices].

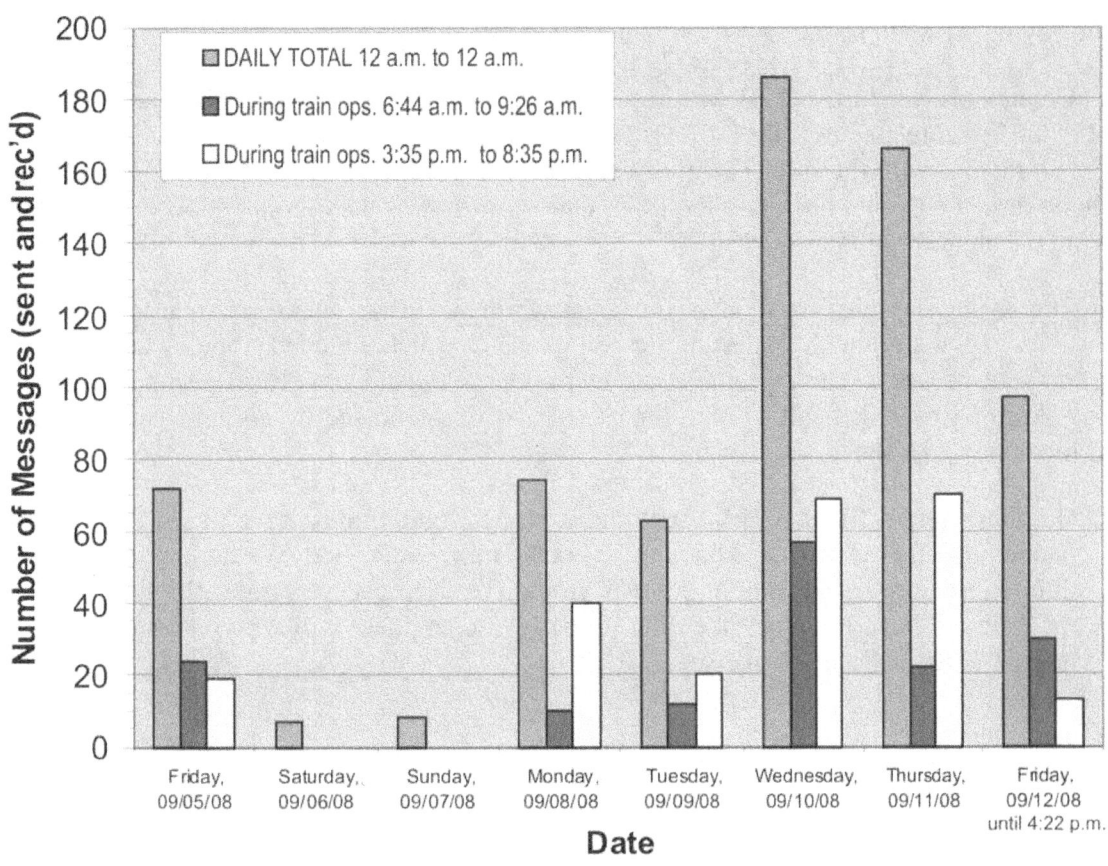

Figure 11. Telephone calls sent and received by Metrolink engineer on day of accident and on previous 7 days.

Also at the public hearing, the safety and operating practices manager stated that on one other occasion he had taken exception to the accident engineer's use of a wireless device while on duty. He said the incident occurred on September 7, 2006, shortly after the policy regarding use of electronic devices by train crews had gone into effect. Several Metrolink, UP, and Amtrak officers performed a joint "blitz" test in the Glendale and Burbank area to identify any possible problems regarding the use of electronic devices and to remind employees of the policy. The tests involved riding trains, stopping and boarding trains, and interviewing employees.

The manager stated that he boarded the engineer's train at Burbank and arranged to have another manager call the engineer's cell phone.[45] The phone, which was in the engineer's briefcase, began ringing while the manager and engineer were conducting a job briefing in the train's operating compartment. The manager said he told the engineer that he was in violation of the policy and that the violation would be entered into the company's efficiency test reporting

---

[45] According to testimony at the public hearing on this accident, Connex used this method of detecting prohibited use of a wireless device until the issuance of Federal Emergency Order 26 (discussed later in this report) on October 7, 2008.

system. He said the engineer told him that he was aware of the policy but that he had forgotten to turn the device off when he had stowed it that morning.

Connex provided the NTSB with results of crewmember efficiency tests conducted since June 25, 2005, that related to Rule 1.10. Of the 14 recorded observations, 10 resulted in citations for noncompliance with the rule. Three observations involved a crewmember having a personal cell phone turned on while operating the train. One of those was the aforementioned observation involving the engineer in this accident.

The manager stated that, after the Chatsworth accident, Metrolink management had become "very aggressive with inspecting for cell phones," which included stopping and boarding trains en route between stations rather than at station stops and closely inspecting trains and crews. Asked if it was difficult to monitor use of a wireless device by an engineer alone in a locked locomotive, he stated:

> Oh, that's very difficult. ...[A]s the train went by, you'd almost have to see a cell phone up to their ear. You'd have to board the train undetected. We do board the train en route from [a] station, but it is very difficult to get on a train. I'll get on the train, I'll have to unlock the door. Usually, the engineer will see you coming. It's extremely difficult to oversee.

Content of Text Messages

Verizon records for the 7 days prior to the day of the accident included the content of most of the text messages sent and received by the Metrolink engineer. Most of the text messages during the engineer's morning trip on the day of the accident appear to be to and from a coworker discussing some type of company correspondence. Six messages were to or from Person A. All of the messages during the afternoon (accident) trip were to or from Person A. These messages appear to be primarily discussing train schedules, how far behind schedule certain trains are, and where different trains may or may not "meet" (pass one another) along the track.

A review of the content of all of the engineer's text messages over the previous 7 days (including those during and outside the times the engineer was responsible for operating a train) indicated that the engineer and Person A had been coordinating to allow Person A to operate train 111 on the evening of the accident, starting at about 7:45 p.m. The intent was for Person A to board the train at Moorpark and to operate it from Moorpark to Montalvo. A portion of one exchange on September 8, 2008, (the Monday before the Friday accident) reads:

[Engineer to Person A]: yea....but I'm REALLY looking forward to getting you in the cab and showing you how to run a locomotive.

[Person A to Engineer]: Omg dude me too. Running a locomotive. Having all of that in the palms of my hands. Its a great feeling. And ill do it so good from all my practice on the simulator.

[Engineer to person A]: I'm gonna do all the radio talkin'...ur gonna run the locomotive & I'm gonna tell u how to do it.

Additionally, Person A and the engineer had arranged for a "ride-along" on the evening of Tuesday, September 9. Person A and Person B were to board the engineer's train at Chatsworth and ride it to Union Station, which they apparently did. The text messages concerning this "ride-along" were not as detailed as those outlining the plans to allow Person A to operate the train; however, messages on the following day (September 10) indicate that Person A was "up in the cab" and "touching the controls." In the same context of the previous evening's activities, the engineer referred to "how much [Person C] wanted to stay in the seat."

On the morning of September 10, the engineer sent to Person B a message that read: "[Person B] you wanna run again tonight to montalvo??? if you can?" Later, another message to Person B read: "this time I'm taking a picture of you @ da throttle!!!" A subsequent message from the engineer to Person B read, "... we should have the 866 this evening...," referencing the locomotive unit number. Person B responded, "A bit tougher to get in and out of the cab but it should be fine".

A number of messages between Person A and the engineer on the day of the accident, as well as on the days leading up to the accident, addressed concerns that the riders would be seen either entering the locomotive or while occupying the cab. Apparently, on the afternoon of the accident, the engineer e-mailed Person A with the plan for boarding the train at Moorpark, to which Person A responded:

[Person A to Engineer]:   Very crafty. Looks good man. And i will have my cell phone.

About 6 minutes later, Person A messaged:

[Person A to Engineer]:   Ok got it printed out. Makes perfect sence [*sic*]. I think you'll
                          be on the main.

Connex Metrolink Notice No. 17.08, dated July 8, 2008, states:

Head End Authorization:

Only the engineer of record, conductor of record, mechanical riders, operating managers and others with proper written authorization are permitted on the head end and/or control compartment of Metrolink trains.

The last message received by the engineer from Person A arrived at the engineer's wireless device at 4:20:57, about the time train 111 was accelerating out of Chatsworth station. Content of that message was as follows: "I would like that too [referring to a possible meet with other trains, the topic of a previous text message]. We already need to meet 796. That would be best." At 4:22:01, about 22 seconds before the collision, the Verizon network recorded that the engineer had sent the following response to Person A: "yea...usually @ north camarillo."

Leesdale Local Conductor's Use of a Wireless Device

Information came to light after the accident to the effect that the Leesdale Local's conductor may have been using a wireless device during the time he was responsible for the operation of his train. To follow up on this information, NTSB investigators obtained the

Verizon Wireless records for the conductor's account. These records include the time and date of incoming and outgoing telephone calls, as well as the time and date of text messages sent and received. The content of the text messages was not available because the date of the request for the records was beyond Verizon's standard retention period for those records.

The Leesdale Local's conductor made three telephone calls while on duty on the day of the accident. These calls appear to be business-related, as they were all to a telephone number associated with the issuance of Metrolink track warrants (authorizations for a train to occupy a certain segment of track for a certain period of time).

The records indicate that the conductor sent or received a total of 41 text messages while on duty between 11:30 a.m. and 4:20 p.m. on the day of the accident. According to the "Conductor's Report," the conductor was on a moving train between 12:29 p.m. and 1:55 p.m., and again from 3:13 p.m. until the accident at 4:22 p.m. During this time, the conductor sent or received a total of 35 text messages. His last outgoing text message was received and logged by the Verizon network at 4:20 p.m., about the time his train exited tunnel 26 and passed signal 4426.

At the public hearing on this accident, the UP general manager of operating practices stated that the conductor's efficiency test records covering the previous 12 months showed no exceptions with regard to his use of electronic devices. At the time many of the text messages were sent, including the last one transmitted about 2 minutes before the collision, the conductor was occupying the locomotive cab along with the engineer. In postaccident interviews, the engineer did not mention that the conductor had used such a device on the day of the accident. Asked at the public hearing what action an employee should take in such a circumstance, the general manager of operating practices stated:

> A fellow crewmember should remind the employee of the rule requirement and tell them they need to turn the cell phone off to be in compliance to the rule. We would expect that of any manager onboard; we certainly would expect it between two crewmembers.

Tests and Research

Sight-Distance Tests of Trains

For the sight-distance tests, exemplar locomotives simulating those of the Metrolink and UP trains were positioned facing each other at the point of collision. The locomotives were then moved away from each other in intervals of 60 feet (representing the approximate distance a 40-mph train will travel in 1 second) until the engineer aboard each locomotive could not see the other train. These tests revealed that each engineer's first view of the opposing train would have occurred when the trains were about 540 feet apart. At that point, at a closing speed of about 80 mph, the trains would have been 4 to 5 seconds from impact. (See figure 12.)

Figure 12. View from the head end of a simulated Leesdale Local during train sight-distance testing. At a closing speed in excess of 80 mph, the trains would be only seconds from impact as the Metrolink train becomes visible around the curve.

Sight-Distance Tests of Signals

Investigators also conducted sight-distance tests for the signals train 111 encountered before arriving at Chatsworth station as well as for the signal display and switch point configuration at CP Topanga.

Signal Aspects East of CP Topanga. For each test of the signals east of CP Topanga, a Metrolink train consist was moved westbound (toward the signal) until the test engineer affirmed that he had a clear view of the signal aspect. The tests confirmed that the aspect of signal 4483 (the westbound signal immediately before CP Bernson), could be seen and identified from 1,832 feet. The aspect of the westbound signal at CP Bernson could be seen and identified from 5,353 feet. Signal 4451 (the intermediate signal train 111 encountered before entering Chatsworth station) could be seen and identified from 1,360 feet.

Signal Aspect at CP Topanga. The westbound signal at CP Topanga consists of a three-aspect (green, yellow, red) signal head on a mast. Each aspect is 8 3/8 inches in diameter. The centers of the yellow and green lenses are 21 feet 6 inches above the ground. The center of the red lens is 20 feet 5 inches above the ground. The control compartment of a locomotive typically positioned at the Chatsworth station is about 5,288 feet from the signal.

The conductor of train 111 told investigators that, just before the train departed Chatsworth station, he could see the CP Topanga signal, and the signal aspect was green. Three individuals—a station security guard and two rail fans—who were on the station platform at the time (and who were on a first-name basis with both the engineer and conductor of train 111) also stated that they had seen the Topanga signal displaying a green aspect after train 111 left the station. One of the rail fans told investigators that the CP Topanga signal was not readily visible from the Chatsworth station platform. He said the signal could be seen if one were to approach the edge of the platform and "lean out," and that this is what he had done as train 111 departed the station on the day of the accident. One of the rail fans also told investigators that it had been his experience at the Chatsworth station that it was not possible to see a red signal at CP Topanga in the daytime, only at night.

On September 15, 2008, the NTSB conducted sight-distance tests of the signal to assess overall visibility of the signal from the vantage point of the Metrolink train conductor and engineer and to determine if ambient light conditions, reflections, or atmospheric conditions could affect an observer's interpretation of the signal aspects. These observations were carried out at the same time of day as the accident.

For the tests, the Metrolink dispatcher aligned the CP Topanga switch for eastbound movement into the siding (as it was on the day of the accident) so that the westbound signal at CP Topanga would display a *stop* indication. About 4:20 p.m., investigators made unaided visual observations of the signal from the conductor's position on the platform as well as from the platform adjacent to the point at which the train 111 locomotive would have been positioned. Some observers reported seeing an intermittently visible "faint glimmer" of red; other observers reported seeing nothing.

About 4:30 p.m., investigators boarded the cab of a three-car Metrolink train while it was positioned at its typical spot alongside the Chatsworth station platform. The Metrolink engineer who participated in the test stated that he could see the signal at Topanga, but he noted that he knew where to look through experience.

The engineer was instructed to depart the station westbound as he normally would and to stop at the point where he could clearly distinguish the red CP Topanga signal. The engineer stopped short of the first road crossing (Devonshire Avenue) and said that he could clearly see the signal. Some members of the observation group reported seeing the signal clearly, while others reported still seeing only an intermittently visible flickering red. At this point the train had traveled 953 feet from the station and was still 4,335 feet from the signal.

The train was then backed up and spotted normally at Chatsworth station. The Metrolink dispatcher aligned CP Topanga for the train's movement westbound in order to have the CP Topanga signal display a green aspect (*clear* indication). At 4:45 p.m., the signal displayed a flashing yellow aspect (*advance approach* indication) that was clearly visible to all observers both in the locomotive cab and in the cab control car.

At 4:46 p.m., the CP Topanga signal displayed a green aspect that again was clearly visible to all observers. At 4:51 p.m., the signal displayed a red aspect. The red signal was faint and only intermittently visible from both the locomotive cab and the conductor's position in the cab control car. Not all observers were able to see this signal aspect.

CP Topanga Switch Alignment. To test visibility of the position of the switch points at the CP Topanga switch, investigators had an engineer back a Metrolink consist eastbound until he could no longer see the position of the switch points. This distance was determined to be about 615 feet.

Testing of Signal System

Postaccident inspection of the signal system found that all signal units and signal cases at the intermediate signals and at the control points Topanga, Bernson, and Davis were locked and sealed with no indications of tampering or vandalism to any of the signal equipment. Investigators examining the signal head of the westbound CP Topanga signal found the signal head to be clean internally with all electrical wiring and connections intact and in good overall condition. The signal head was found to be sealed against external light sources.

Mechanical and electrical tests were performed on all switch and signal components at CP Topanga. The tests confirmed that, except for components damaged as a result of the accident, all switch and signal components worked as designed. Testing of the Vital Harmon Logic Controller confirmed that conflicting routes could not be cleared simultaneously.

The Metrolink dispatch center aligned the route as it was at the time of the accident,[46] and investigators used rolling shunts[47] to simulate the movements of Metrolink train 111 and the Leesdale Local. Signal personnel positioned at CP Davis, at intermediate signal 4426; at the east- and westbound signals at CP Topanga, at intermediate signal 4451, and at CP Bernson confirmed that the signal system functioned as designed and intended.

While the route was aligned for an eastbound train movement into the siding at CP Topanga, investigators, as a test, sent a request for the westbound Topanga signal to clear. The Harmon Vital Logic Controller at that location would not act on this command, and the westbound signal did not clear. The controller is designed to ensure that lamp output energy is in compliance with the requested signal aspect and that an internal or external fault will not result in an improperly displayed signal. With the eastbound signal at Topanga displaying *clear*, investigators applied battery power to the green signal lamp of the westbound signal. Within 1 second, the Harmon Vital Logic Controller detected the improperly illuminated lamp and, as designed, changed the eastbound Topanga signal from *clear* to *stop* and started a 6-minute timer, which effectively locked out the control point and prevented any commands from being acted upon.

---

[46] On the day of the accident, the dispatcher had stacked the route for the westbound movement; on the day of the testing, the westbound route requests were not stacked.

[47] *Shunting* the track refers to connecting the two rails electrically to simulate the presence of a train. With a *rolling shunt*, shunts are installed then repositioned in a pattern that simulates a train's movement along a block of track.

As an additional test, investigators had the CP Topanga switch aligned for eastbound movement into the siding and locked. They then initiated a request to clear the Topanga westbound signal. This test was performed once with the eastbound signal displaying *clear* and again with the signal displaying *stop*. The logic controller would not act on either command and did not clear the westbound signal.

The validity of the downloaded signal event recorder data was confirmed by a review of recordings from the forward-looking video camera of the Leesdale Local, which showed that all signals encountered by the Local were displaying their proper aspects as indicated by the signal recorder data.

Examination of the Metrolink signal data log and signal maintenance records did not identify any condition that would have prevented the signal system from operating as designed. Signal trouble reports for the 6 months preceding the accident were reviewed, and no exceptions were noted for the westbound signal at CP Topanga.

Testing of Communications System

On September 17, 2008, three communications tests were conducted to determine whether communication "dead spots" existed along the route of Metrolink train 111 that would have interfered with radio transmissions between train crewmembers or that would have prevented radio transmissions from being recorded by the dispatch center. All the tests were conducted using handheld radios, including the radio that was in the possession of the train 111 conductor on the day of the accident.[48]

The first test involved making radio transmissions every 2 minutes from on board an exemplar train as it traveled eastbound from the Simi Valley station to the Northridge station. The second test was the same as the first except that the train was traveling westbound from Northridge to Simi Valley. The dispatch center confirmed that the communications were successful, with the only exception being a loss of communication inside tunnel 26.

The final test was done on the ground east and west of CP Topanga. The test was distance-based and was designed to evaluate communication between the handheld radio and the dispatch center. The only failed communications noted were within 100 feet of the portal of tunnel 28.

The handheld radio being used by the conductor of Metrolink train 111 on the day of the accident was determined to be fully functional. Testing of the handset battery revealed that when fully charged, the battery lost capacity over a relatively short period of time, which reduced the radio's transmit power. Testing showed that after three to five talk cycles, the audible low-battery warning activated at the end of each subsequent talk cycle.

---

[48] The in-cab radio the train 111 engineer used for all his radio transmissions on the day of the accident was destroyed in the accident and was therefore not available for testing.

Inspection and Testing of Track

Investigators made postaccident inspections of the track geometry west of CP Topanga and took measurements at a total of 25 stations in the undisturbed track to the east of the point of collision. (No measurements were taken to the west of the point of collision because of disturbances to the track as a result of the accident and the subsequent repair work.) The measurements revealed track conditions as follows:

Track Gage. Widest gage (distance between the inside faces of the running rails) was measured at 56 7/8 inches. FRA Track Safety Standards permit a maximum gage of 57 3/4 inches in class 3 track.

Track Alignment. The maximum alignment (relative positions of the two rails laterally) deviation in undisturbed track measured 5/16 inch. FRA Track Safety Standards permit a maximum deviation of 1 3/4 inch in class 3 track.

Cross Level. Greatest deviation in cross level (difference from the specified elevation between the two rails) was measured as 5/16 inch. FRA Track Safety Standards permit a maximum deviation of 1 11/16 inch in class 3 track.

Overall, no unacceptable conditions were found in the geometry of the track.

Other Information

Postaccident Actions by SCRRA

According to SCRRA representatives, after the accident, SCRRA put into place a *Metrolink Enhanced Safety Action Plan* that incorporates the following elements:

Safety Culture

- Elevated the Safety Department to report directly to the SCRRA chief executive officer (CEO), with safety manager required to meet with CEO at least weekly, to provide CEO with monthly written updates, and to provide the SCRRA board with quarterly updates.

- Created a Strategic Safety Leadership Team comprising all operating general managers, SCRRA contract managers, and the CEO. The leadership team:

  - Meets quarterly with the goal of sharing information on common problems, on best practices, and on future safety efforts by SCRRA.

  - Reviews safety performance by SCRRA and its contactors

- Established a risk-assessment process.

- Is developing goals with regard to training, efficiency testing, rules violations, injuries, audits/inspections.

SCRRA Organizational Structure

- Hired an assistant director of equipment.

- Hired a manager of field operations and three operations compliance officers.

- Established a new field operation unit responsible for efficiency testing of foreign line trains operating over SCRRA territory as well as performing oversight testing of the SCRRA contract operator.

- Created a System Safety Committee structure that involves all organizational layers, including contractors.

Metrolink Operations

- Updated the Metrolink operational testing program.

- Hired an operating rules manager responsible for implementing the updated efficiency testing program.

- Increased observations of engineers, conductors, and other safety-critical employees as well as increased joint testing with other operators on the territory.

- Installed inward- and forward-facing cameras on its locomotives to monitor engineers for compliance with rules regarding electronic devices, unauthorized personnel in the operating compartment, and sleeping, and has established a program for the routine reviewing of the recorded images.[49]

Metrolink Safety Projects

- Accelerating the development and deployment of positive train control on the Metrolink locomotive fleet by December 2012 and the installation of positive train control on SCRRA territory by 2015.

  - Has reassigned staff and hired 40 additional contract employees to oversee the installation of positive train control, which includes a new dispatch system, installation of the back office servers (BOS), retrofitting of the locomotive and cab car fleet for the new micro-processors and new video screens, training and hiring of additional staff to support positive train control, re-spacing of signals, and the development of algorithms for stopping distances of commuter equipment.

  - Is working with the FRA and the railroad industry on communication, equipment and operating rules in advance of the December 2012 commitment.

---

[49] The Brotherhood of Locomotive Engineers and Trainmen has filed suit in U.S. District Court to prohibit SCRRA from using its in-cab audio and video system for this purpose.

- Has installed 43 additional Inert Inductor Automatic Train Stop systems to alert engineers to the need to reduce speed. The inert inductors require that the engineer acknowledge a reduced speed requirement of 20 mph or more within 8 seconds or receive a penalty brake application.

- Is purchasing Crash Energy Management cab control cars and trailer cars that will be placed in operation starting in 2010. These cars will have crash-energy seats, frangible tables, and push-back couplers. The existing fleet will be retrofitted with crash energy seats, push-back couplers, and frangible tables.

- Is installing new LED lights at all control point signals, to be completed in 2010.

Federal Rules Regarding Wireless Devices

In its investigation of a May 28, 2002, collision of two Burlington Northern Santa Fe freight trains near Clarendon, Texas,[50] the NTSB determined the probable cause of the accident to be, in part, "the coal train engineer's use of a cell phone during the time he should have been attending to the requirements of the track warrant for his train." As a result of that investigation, the NTSB made the following safety recommendation to the FRA:

R-03-1
Promulgate new or amended regulations that will control the use of cellular telephones and similar wireless communication devices by railroad operating employees while on duty so that such use does not affect operational safety.

In its October 2003 response to this recommendation, the FRA stated its belief that the railroad industry's establishment and enforcement of its own operating rules governing cell phone use were sufficient to address the issue without the need for Federal action. The FRA also noted that it would continue to "closely monitor railroad compliance with their operating rules restricting cell phone use and will not hesitate to take appropriate enforcement action if it becomes necessary."

During a March 2004 meeting with NTSB staff, FRA representatives indicated that the agency had issued instructions to FRA staff to be mindful of their own use of cell phones, but they suggested that enforcing a Federal rule would be almost impossible. The FRA did, however, refer the issue to its Railroad Safety Advisory Committee for discussion as to whether the issue should be addressed by a new safety advisory committee working group. Based on this response, Safety Recommendation R-03-1 was initially classified "Open—Acceptable Response."

When the issue of a new or amended Federal regulation was subsequently brought before the Railroad Safety Advisory Committee, the members agreed that the complexity of the issue was such that the committee was not prepared at that time to consider a Federal rule. On March 7, 2007, the NTSB, noting that little progress had been made in almost 3 1/2 years from the date

---

[50] *Collision of Two Burlington Northern Santa Fe Freight Trains Near Clarendon, Texas May 28, 2002,* Railroad Accident Report NTSB/RAR-03/01 (Washington, DC: National Transportation Safety Board, 2003).

the recommendation was issued, reclassified Safety Recommendation R-03-1 "Open—Unacceptable Response." Thus, at the time of the accident, no Federal rail regulations prohibited the use of cell phones or similar devices by train crewmembers.

On October 7, 2008, after and in response to the Chatsworth accident, the FRA issued Emergency Order 26, *Emergency Order To Restrict On-Duty Railroad Operating Employees' Use of Cellular Telephones and Other Distracting Electronic and Electrical Devices,*[51] which details the circumstances under which train crewmembers could use both company-supplied and personal electronic devices.

With regard to personal electronic devices, Emergency Order 26 states:

(c) Personal electronic and electrical devices. (1) Each personal electronic or electrical device must be turned off with any earpieces removed from the ear while on a moving train, except that, when radio failure occurs, a wireless communication device may be used in accordance with railroad rules and instructions.

(2) Each personal electronic or electrical device must be turned off with any earpieces removed from the ear when a duty requires any railroad operating employee to be on the ground or to ride rolling equipment during a switching operation and during any period when another employee of the railroad is assisting in preparation of the train (e.g., during an air brake test).

(3) Use of a personal electronic or electrical device to perform any function other than voice communication while on duty is prohibited. In no instance may a personal electronic or electrical device interfere with the railroad operating employee's performance of safety-related duties.

Because Emergency Order 26 met the intent of Safety Recommendation R-03-1, the NTSB, on September 17, 2009, reclassified recommendation R-03-1 "Closed—Acceptable Alternate Action" At the same time, the NTSB expressed its disappointment that the FRA had not taken previous action on this important safety recommendation.

FRA Emergency Order 20 (1996)

On February 20, 1996, in the wake of fatal collisions involving commuter trains near Secaucus, New Jersey,[52] and Silver Spring, Maryland,[53] the FRA issued Emergency Order 20, Notice No. 1, *Emergency Order Requiring Enhanced Operating Rules and Plans for Ensuring*

---

[51] *Federal Register*, vol. 73, no. 195 (October 7, 2008), p. 58702.

[52] *Near Head-On Collision and Derailment of Two New Jersey Transit Trains Near Secaucus, New Jersey, February 9, 1996*, Railroad Accident Report NTSB/RAR-97/01 (Washington, DC: National Transportation Safety Board, 1997).

[53] *Collision and Derailment of Maryland Rail Commuter MARC Train 286 and National Railroad Passenger Corporation Amtrak Train 29 Near Silver Spring, Maryland, on February 16, 1996*, Railroad Accident Report NTSB/RAR-97/02 (Washington, DC: National Transportation Safety Board, 1997).

the Safety of Passengers Occupying the Leading Car of a Train. The emergency order imposed rule enhancements involving compliance with signal indications and addressed issues related to passenger safety and emergency egress. As refined by Emergency Order 20, Notice No. 2, issued on March 5, 1996, the order required that commuter and intercity passenger railroads issue an operating rule as follows:

> (A) If a passenger train operating in the block immediately preceding an interlocking or controlled point stops for any reason, [including a station stop] or its speed is reduced below 10 m.p.h., the train shall proceed under the reduced speed set forth in applicable operating rules governing such circumstances and be prepared to stop before passing the next signal. In no event shall this reduced speed exceed 40 m.p.h., although lower speeds are permissible. The train must maintain the prescribed reduced speed until the next wayside signal is clearly visible and that signal displays a proceed indication.

The order further required that:

> (E) Within 30 days of issuance of the railroad's rule, an appropriate qualifying appurtenance shall be affixed to each signal governing the approach to an interlocking or controlled point signal to serve as a visual reminder to the engineer. Appropriate signage shall be displayed at the departure end of passenger stations located in the block immediately preceding interlockings or controlled points.

At the time the FRA issued Emergency Order 20, Metrolink operating rules included the following:

9.9: Train Delayed Within a Block

If a train has entered a block on a proceed indication that does not require restricted speed, and the train stops or its speed is reduced below 10 MPH, the train must:

...B. CTC or Manual Interlocking Limits

Proceed prepared to stop at the next signal until the next signal is visible and that signal displays a proceed indication.

Passenger trains operating in push/pull service must not exceed 40 MPH until the next signal is visible and that signal displays a proceed indication.

Based on Operating Rule 9.9, Metrolink petitioned the FRA for relief from the signage requirement of the emergency order. On April 30, 1996, the FRA granted Metrolink the waiver:

> conditioned on the fact that the current operating rules require compliance with the delayed-in-block rule by all trains, in all blocks, at all times. Under these circumstances, FRA agrees that the placement of signage required by EO 20 could send a mixed and confusing message to operating crews concerning the application of the rule.

Analysis

Exclusions

Based on UP and Connex records, the crewmembers of both the Metrolink and UP trains were experienced railroaders fully qualified to perform their duties. Examination of the work/rest histories of all crewmembers did not indicate that any crewmember was experiencing fatigue that would have affected performance before or at the time of the accident. The engineer and brakeman on the Leesdale Local were on their regular assignment and, for several days before the accident, had gone on duty at 11:30 a.m. and off duty at 6:30 or 7:00 p.m., thus experiencing consistent work/rest patterns to which they were accustomed. The train's conductor was an extra employee filling in for the regularly assigned conductor. He had worked the Leesdale Local on Monday before the accident and had been off Tuesday, Wednesday, and Thursday before being called to work the Leesdale Local again on Friday. He had maintained a fairly consistent wake/rest cycle during his days off.

The Metrolink train 111 engineer had also maintained the same work schedule for the 4 days leading up to the accident, going on duty at 5:54 a.m. and working until 9:26 a.m., then returning for the second part of his shift at 2:00 p.m. and working until 9:05 p.m. On the day of the accident, according to the conductor on the Metrolink train, the engineer said he had taken a nap during his mid-day break and was well rested when he reported for work for his afternoon tour of duty.

Based on the operator's height and weight at the time of his last physical examination, he had a calculated body mass index (BMI) of 34.4. By this calculation, the operator would have been considered obese (a BMI greater than 30 constitutes obesity). Obesity is significantly associated with an increased risk for obstructive sleep apnea (OSA), which can result in fatigue and significant cognitive and psychomotor deficits. In addition, the engineer had previously noted possible snoring and was noted on autopsy to have enlargement of the chambers of his heart. Right-sided heart chamber enlargement, in particular, has been associated with severe sleep-disordered breathing (including OSA).[54] However, the engineer had not been evaluated for or diagnosed with sleep apnea, and he remained actively engaged in operating his train during his afternoon shift, including making regular station stops and calling out some, though not all, of the signals the train encountered along its route. During the approximately 2 minutes that elapsed between the time train 111 departed Chatsworth station until the accident, the engineer was engaged in text messaging, manipulating the throttle, sounding the train horn and bell, and making brake adjustments, with no period of inactivity that might have suggested a lack of alertness due to fatigue or lack of sleep.

---

[54] U. C. Guidry, L. A. Mendes, J. C. Evans, D. Levy, G. T. O'Connor, M. G. Larson, D. J. Gottlieb, E. J. Benjamin. "Echocardiographic Features of the Right Heart in Sleep-Disordered Breathing: The Framingham Heart Study," *American Journal of Respiratory and Critical Care Medicine.* 164(6) September 15(2001):933-8.

The engineer had a history of diabetes and high blood pressure and had been taking prescription medications for these conditions. He had also tested HIV positive and was being treated with anti-retroviral medications. According to his medical records, his conditions were under good control, and no adverse side effects were reported from his medication use.

Information downloaded from event recorders aboard the locomotives of the Leesdale Local indicated that the train had been operated in accordance with signal indications from the time it entered the main track at CP Davis until the accident. Correlation between event recorder and sight-distance data indicate that emergency braking was applied 1 to 2 seconds after Metrolink train 111 came into view, but the time and distance were insufficient for the braking to have prevented or reduced the severity of the accident.

Postaccident toxicological tests were conducted on each crewmember of the Leesdale Local, as well as the conductor of the Metrolink train 111. Specimens were also obtained from the engineer of train 111. Except for those of the UP conductor, all specimens were negative for the presence of alcohol as well as for FRA-specified illicit drugs.

The UP conductor tested negative for alcohol but was positive for marijuana in both his blood and urine. The relative amounts of tetrahydrocannabinol (the active substance in marijuana) and its metabolite suggest use within about 12 to 20 hours of the blood being drawn.[55] Based on the reported times the blood and urine specimens were taken, the conductor likely used marijuana within 3 to 11 hours of the accident. If so, it is possible that he was impaired at the time of the accident.[56] However, the Leesdale Local was being operated in compliance with signal indications on its approach to the siding at Chatsworth; thus the conductor's marijuana use was not a factor in the accident.

After the accident, the cars of both trains that had not been destroyed in the accident were inspected and tested. Air brake and mechanical tests confirmed that the equipment was in good working order, with no anomalies noted that would have contributed to the accident. Similarly, the track segment train 111 traversed in the moments before the accident was found to be in good condition, with all track geometry measurements falling within Federal tolerances for that class of track.

It was daylight at the time of the accident. The weather was warm with clear skies and calm winds. Although some haze was present, visibility was reported as 4 miles. Thus, no meteorological conditions existed that would have impaired the train crews' vision with regard to signal aspects or that would have otherwise affected train operations.

---

[55] Based on data in M. A. Huestis, J. E. Henningfield, E. J. Cone. "Blood Cannabinoids. II. Models for the Prediction of Time of Marijuana Exposure from Plasma Concentrations of Delta 9-Tetrahydrocannabinol (THC) and 11-Nor-9-Carboxy-Delta 9-Tetrahydrocannabinol (THCCOOH)," *Journal of Analytical Toxicology*. 16(5) Sep-Oct (1992):283-90.

[56] See (a) R. C. Baselt. Drug Effects on Psychomotor Performance (Foster City, California: Biomedical Publications, 2001). (b) V. O. Leirer, J. A. Yesavage, D. G. Morrow. "Marijuana Carry-Over Effects on Aircraft Pilot Performance," *Aviation, Space, and Environmental Medicine*. 62(3) March (1991):221-7. (c) J. A. Yesavage, V. O. Leirer, M. Denari, L. E. Hollister. "Carry-Over Effects of Marijuana Intoxication on Aircraft Pilot Performance: A Preliminary Report," *American Journal of Psychiatry*. 142(11) Nov (1985): 1325-9.

The NTSB therefore concludes that the following were neither causal nor contributory to this accident: weather, fatigue, the engineer's medical conditions or treatments, training and experience of crewmembers, operation of UP Leesdale Local, alcohol or illegal drug use by operating crewmembers, and condition of the track or rolling stock. The NTSB further concludes that although the conductor of the UP Leesdale Local had likely used marijuana within 3 to 11 hours of the accident, this was neither causal nor contributory to the accident.

The Accident

On the afternoon of September 12, 2008, the Leesdale Local had completed its work and was headed eastbound to its home terminal at Gemco. At the same time, Metrolink train 111 was on its scheduled westbound run from Los Angeles Union Station to Montalvo. The two trains would be using the same track, meaning that at some point one of the trains would have to divert into a siding track and wait for the other to pass before it could continue its trip. Deciding when, where, and how opposing trains will meet is the job of the dispatcher.

In this case, the dispatcher decided to allow the eastbound Leesdale Local to enter the main track at CP Davis while westbound train 111 was still east of CP Topanga on the same track. The dispatcher planned to have the freight train proceed to CP Topanga where it would divert from the main track through the siding at Chatsworth. As soon as this move was complete, train 111 would be able to continue westbound.

At 4:07:37 p.m., according to signal data logs, the switch at CP Topanga responded to the dispatcher's request and "reversed," that is, aligned to force any eastbound train to move onto the siding track rather than continue on the main track. The switch was now aligned *against* a westbound train movement on the main track. The switch and signal circuitry for the controlling westbound CP Topanga signal was designed such that, with the switch reversed, the westbound signal could display no aspect other than red, or *stop*, for westbound trains.

With this first route programmed in, the dispatcher "stacked" the next route commands in the sequence, requesting that the CP Topanga switch realign for the main track and that the westbound signal clear for a westbound train movement after the freight train was fully in the siding.

The signal system is designed such that a red aspect at westbound CP Topanga causes the westbound signal at CP Bernson to display a flashing yellow aspect (*advance approach* indication) and intermediate signal 4451 just east of Chatsworth station to display solid yellow (*approach* indication) to approaching trains. Train 111's engineer was recorded calling out the flashing yellow signal at CP Bernson. He was not recorded calling out intermediate signal 4451 or the next signal, CP Topanga.

As train 111 departed Chatsworth station, the engineer proceeded as though the signal at CP Topanga were green (*clear*) even though the flashing yellow at CP Bernson (which he definitely saw and called) and the solid yellow at intermediate signal 4451 indicated that, at the time train 111 passed them, the CP Topanga signal was displaying a red aspect. Even if intermediate signal 4451 had been green, indicating that the signal at CP Topanga was, at that time, also green, Metrolink's delay-in-block rule would have required that the engineer leave

Chatsworth station and proceed at no more than 40 mph until he could confirm the indication at CP Topanga. Instead, the engineer accelerated his train to 54 mph.

About 2 minutes after leaving Chatsworth station, train 111 ran through and damaged the CP Topanga switch, which had been aligned against westbound travel. At the time his train ran through the switch, the engineer was not able to see the Leesdale Local advancing toward him. His first possible view of the freight train would have occurred as his train entered the left-hand curve just west of the switch. According to the locomotive data recorder, the engineer did not apply the train brakes before impact. The Leesdale Local crew did promptly apply brakes on their train when train 111 came into their view, but it was not possible to significantly slow the train in the seconds that elapsed before the collision.

Emergency Response

Emergency responders arrived at the scene of the accident shortly after the initial notification, and a unified command system was established with the responding agencies and the railroads. Mutual aid resources were also requested from surrounding areas. During the course of the response, the incident commander established a fire suppression group, an extrication group, a medical group, a hazardous materials group, and an urban search and rescue group. Firefighters, police officers, sheriff's deputies, and highway patrol officers worked to rescue, triage, and transport injured passengers and train crew. About 1,000 emergency personnel responded.

As a result of the collision, the rear end of the locomotive telescoped into about two-thirds of the first passenger coach, causing a complete loss of survivable occupant space. Because of this damage, the extrication of passengers from the first coach was a difficult and dangerous operation that required extensive manpower, resources, and time. Despite the difficulties, responders carried out their duties as quickly and as efficiently as could be expected. The NTSB therefore concludes that, considering the challenges of the recovery operations, the emergency response to the accident was timely, well coordinated, and effectively managed.

As a result of the collision, fuel spilled from the Metrolink locomotive, and a fire burned near the locomotives. During the firefighters' fire suppression operations, they discovered that two crewmembers were trapped inside the cab of the lead locomotive on the Leesdale Local. The cab was filled with smoke. Firefighters eventually forced entry into the cab through a window and rescued the crew, both of whom had suffered serious injuries. The NTSB concludes that because locomotive cab exits are not designed to be quickly opened in an emergency, firefighters could not rapidly enter the cab of the Leesdale Local to rescue the injured crew.

The NTSB addressed this issue during its investigation of a November 30, 2007, collision of an Amtrak passenger train and a Norfolk Southern Railway Company freight train near Chicago, Illinois.[57] In that collision, the forward portion of the Amtrak locomotive came to rest

---

[57] *Collision of Amtrak Passenger Train 371 and Norfolk Southern Railway Company Freight Train 23M Chicago, Illinois, November 30, 2007*, Railroad Accident Report NTSB/RAR-09/01 (Washington, DC: National Transportation Safety Board, 2009).

on top of a container on the rear car of the freight train. Because of structural damage to the locomotive cab, the two engineers could not exit without assistance. As a result of the accident, the NTSB made the following recommendation to the FRA:

> R-09-3
> Require that emergency exits on new and remanufactured locomotive cabs provide for rapid egress by cab occupants and rapid entry by emergency responders.

The FRA responded in May 2009 that it shares the NTSB's concern about rapid egress and rescue access for locomotive cabs, a concern that had been addressed, in part, through previously issued regulatory design requirements for new locomotives. The FRA has also funded new research into locomotive egress and rescue, to include concepts for a roof-mounted escape hatch and an easily removable windshield system. The FRA further responded that it had developed and provided to local emergency responders a training video titled "Locomotive Emergency Response Operations." Finally, the FRA stated that it would present this recommendation and its actions to date to the Railroad Safety Advisory Committee's Locomotive Standards Working Group for further consideration. Based on this response, the NTSB has classified Safety Recommendation R-09-3 "Open—Acceptable Response."

Signals and Train Control

Signal Aspect at CP Topanga

In postaccident interviews, the train 111 conductor and three other individuals (two rail fans and a security guard) who were on the Chatsworth station platform while the train served the station stated that they had seen the CP Topanga signal as train 111 pulled out of the station and that the signal was displaying a green aspect. Had this signal been displaying green, the engineer's actions after the train departed the station would have been appropriate, at least until he was close enough to the CP Topanga switch to see that the switch was aligned against his train. Had he realized that he was about to run through the switch, he would doubtless have taken action to stop his train even if the signal had been green. But he took no action in his approach to the switch, while running through it, or immediately afterward.

The evidence is incontrovertible that the CP Topanga switch was aligned for an eastbound movement into the siding as westbound train 111 approached and went through it. The damage to the switch points that was found after the accident could only have occurred as a result of a run-through from the westbound direction. If this damage had occurred before the arrival of train 111, the malfunctioning switch would have been detected by the computerized dispatching system and would have shown on the dispatcher's display as being "out of correspondence," a condition that would have caused all the CP Topanga signals to display red.

Once the switch is reversed and the switch points move away by a fraction of an inch from the main track stock rail, the electrical path that would permit the westbound signal to display a green aspect is interrupted, and the system does not allow the westbound signal at CP Topanga to show any aspect other than red. In postaccident signal tests, investigators used an independent power source to illuminate the green lamp in the westbound CP Topanga signal while the eastbound signal was showing *clear* (a green aspect), an action that would have placed the two signals in conflict. Within 1 second, the logic circuits in the signal controller detected the contradiction and responded by changing the eastbound signal from *clear* to *stop* and temporarily locking the signals so that no commands could be acted upon. Even had some unknown anomaly existed that would have permitted the westbound signal to display a green aspect while the switch was reversed, that display would have been recorded on the signal data logs. Instead, the data logs showed that the only signal repeater relay that was energized from the time the switch was reversed until the time of the accident was the relay for the red lamp. The fact that this relay was energized also shows conclusively that the red lamp was actually illuminated, because the current needed to energize this relay must pass through the lamp. If the lamp bulb were missing or burned out, this relay could not have been energized.

Inspection and testing of the lights themselves determined that the signal lamps and lenses were undamaged and operating properly. Signal inspection records indicated no deficiencies that would have prevented proper operation of the signal system. Finally, tests and analysis of the signal event recorders, along with the Metrolink Control Center's Digicon signal event log, determined that the signal aspects were properly displayed and were not in conflict at the time of the accident.

The NTSB therefore concludes that physical evidence, documentary and recorded data, and postaccident signal examination and testing confirm that the westbound signal at CP Topanga was displaying a red aspect at the time Metrolink train 111 departed Chatsworth station and as it approached and passed CP Topanga, and had the engineer complied with this signal indication, the accident would not have occurred.

Stacking of Routes

At the time of the accident, the dispatcher had "stacked" the routes for the Leesdale Local and train 111. Even before the Leesdale Local had completed its planned move, the dispatcher had entered commands to realign the CP Topanga switch and to change the westbound signal to green. But these commands could only be carried out after the previous route had been completed, that is, after the Leesdale Local was in the siding. The investigation determined that the commands to realign the switch and clear the signal were still in the dispatching queue and were never sent to the logic controllers in the field. Had these stacked commands been sent prematurely, the logic controllers would have responded as they did during postaccident testing; that is, they would have sensed a potential routing conflict and changed all the control point signals to red until the conflict could be resolved. The NTSB therefore concludes that the signal and traffic control systems worked as designed on the day of the collision, and the dispatcher's "stacking" of train routes played no role in the accident.

Perceptions of Signal Aspects

Four witnesses at the Chatsworth station stated that they had seen the westbound CP Topanga signal as train 111 left the station and that the signal was displaying a green aspect. But, as previously noted, all the physical and documentary evidence shows conclusively that the signal aspect was red.

The results of postaccident sight-distance tests demonstrated the difficulty in identifying a red signal aspect at CP Topanga when viewed from the Chatsworth station. During that testing, test participants on the station platform were able to identify green and flashing yellow signals but were unable to reliably identify a red signal. The engineer who participated in the sight-distance tests and who, by his own account, "knew where to look," had to move his locomotive almost 1,000 feet from the station before he had what he considered to be a view of the signal adequate to positively identify the signal aspect when it was displaying red, or *stop*. At this distance, some members of the observation group reported that they were still unable to reliably identify the red aspect. These findings were not surprising given that the signal aspect is an 8 3/8-inch-diameter lighted disk almost a mile away being viewed in daylight.

Eyewitness reports of the signal indication at the time of the accident must be evaluated in the context of the physical relationship between the signal and the station, the environmental conditions, and the capabilities and known limitations of the human visual system. The visual angle of the westbound signal light at CP Topanga when viewed from Chatsworth station is essentially equal to the aperture of a single photoreceptor, which puts it near the limit of normal visual function,[58] making it particularly difficult to identify signal color from that distance. An observer with excellent vision who is familiar with the signal and the surrounding environment may be able to see, and perhaps identify the color of, the signal light, but it is more likely that an observer either will not be able to see a signal light at this distance or will misidentify its color. As illustrated by the sight-distance testing results in this investigation, this is particularly true of a red signal aspect because the human visual system is less sensitive to red light than green light.

Research on railroad signal detection has reported misperceptions of signal color at long distances under certain conditions or by certain viewers.[59] However, that research was associated with viewing distances of about 2,950 feet, which is a little more than half the distance from Chatsworth station to CP Topanga. At longer distances, research showed that viewers were often unable to accurately perceive signal color.

The human visual system has been found to be more sensitive to brightness than to color when viewing very small stimuli.[60] That is, the stimulus may be above a person's threshold for perception of brightness but below the threshold for the perception of color, allowing a viewer to

---

[58] Studies of the human retina estimate that at the center of the foveal region—which corresponds roughly to the center of a person's field of view—a single cone photoreceptor in a typical human eye integrates light through an aperture approximately 2.5 µm in diameter, equating to a visual angle of approximately 0.5 arcminutes or .008 degrees. (An arcminute is a unit of angular measurement equal to 1/60 of 1 degree.) The common visual acuity reference of 20/20 is the ability to resolve a high contrast spatial pattern separated by 1 arcminute. For addition information see (a) D. R. Williams. "Topography of the Foveal Cone Mosaic in the Living Human Eye," *Vision Research* 28 (1988): 433-454. (b) C. A. Curcio, K. R. Sloan, R. E. Kalina, and A. E. Hendrickson. "Human Photoreceptor Topography," *Journal of Comparative Neurology* 292 (1990): 497-523. (c) L. N. Thibos. "Formation and Sampling of the Retinal Image," in K. K. De Valois (Ed.) *Seeing* (San Diego, CA: Academic Press, 2000) pp.1-49.

[59] J. M. Wood, D. A. Atchison, and A. Chaparro. "When Red Lights Look Yellow," *Investigative Ophthalmology and Visual Science*. 46(11) (2005): 4348-4352.

[60] P. E. King-Smith and D. Carden. "Luminance and Opponent-Color Contributions to Visual Detection and Adaptation and to Temporal and Spatial Integration." *Journal of the Optical Society of America*. 1976;66:709–717.

perceive a lighted object without being able to identify its color. Consistent with this phenomenon, Wood et al. found that observers could report red railroad signals as still appearing bright at distances from which they could not perceive them as red.[61] In this accident, witnesses viewing the signal from the station under the lighting conditions at the time may have seen the signal, if they saw it at all, as "not red" rather than positively green and may simply have perceived the color they expected. One of the rail fan witnesses who had reported seeing the green signal at CP Topanga acknowledged in his interview that red signals at CP Topanga were not visible during the day, they were visible only at night. Therefore, the NTSB concludes that eyewitness reports of seeing a green aspect from the Chatsworth station are contrary to the other evidence; postaccident testing and research show that witnesses could not have reliably seen the red aspect that the CP Topanga signal was displaying as train 111 departed the station because of a combination of extreme distance to the signal (more than 1 mile), lighting conditions at the time, and limitations of the human visual system.

Performance of Train 111 Engineer

While at the Chatsworth station, the train 111 engineer had a view of the CP Topanga signal that was subject to the same limitations as that of the witnesses on the platform. But unlike the witnesses, this was not the engineer's first clue that the signal might be red, nor was it his last opportunity to observe, identify, and respond to it.

Both the flashing yellow aspect at CP Bernson and the solid yellow aspect at signal 4451 would have indicated to the engineer that the CP Topanga signal was red and that he would have to stop there if the signal did not clear before he reached it. The engineer saw the flashing yellow signal and was recorded calling it out over the radio. He was not recorded calling out the solid yellow signal, so it cannot be confirmed whether he observed it, although he clearly had the opportunity to do so.

Similarly, when train 111 departed Chatsworth station, the engineer had additional opportunities to observe and respond to the signal at CP Topanga. His train was moving during this time, so the signal would have been coming more clearly into his view as he approached it. But he was not recorded calling out this signal over the radio, and he clearly did not respond appropriately to the *stop* indication it was displaying. The engineer's action, or lack of action, with regard to the red stop signal at CP Topanga suggests that he was not fully attentive to his primary task of operating his train safely. He did manipulate the train controls during this time, but these manipulations involved long-practiced and ingrained tasks that he could carry out with little conscious effort and without being particularly focused on his work.

Records from the engineer's cell phone provider show activity on the engineer's wireless device between the time the train left the station and the time of the collision, indicating that the device was on and being used during that period. The records show that at 4:21:03 p.m., or 47 seconds after departing the station, the engineer received a 71-character text message on his wireless device. Sometime within the next minute he responded with a 32-character text message. This was the last text message the engineer sent or received before the collision.

---

[61] Wood, et. al., "When Red Lights Look Yellow,"

Because wireless network records regarding "sent" times are less precise than those regarding "received" times, it cannot be known with certainty at what time the engineer pressed the "send" button on his wireless device to transmit his last message. But the content of the message clearly shows that it was in response to the previous message, which he had received just as the train was pulling out of the station. Thus, during at least part of the time that he could have been, and should have been, observing the signal at CP Topanga, the engineer was likely reading an incoming text message, formulating a response, and entering that response into his wireless device.

Among highway users, text messaging has been shown to have the potential to impose visual, manual, and cognitive demands that greatly exceed those required for voice calls.[62] Furthermore, research has demonstrated that people adjust their reading rate to accommodate the rate at which messages scroll. As the rate of scroll increases, more time is devoted to reading and comprehending the message, making less time available for viewing the roadway.[63]

The train 111 engineer's participation in text messaging after departing Chatsworth station distracted him from adequately attending to a critical task—observing and properly responding to the signal indication at Topanga. He should have known to expect a red signal there because of the flashing yellow signal at CP Bernson that he reported and the solid yellow signal at 4451 he had passed only moments before. He may have thought, or hoped, that the signal would clear before his train reached it, but even this expectation would have required that he proceed while being prepared to stop and that he continue to observe the signal until his train reached it. He did neither. The engineer's operation of the train throttle, bell, and horn after he left the station, as well as his text messaging, indicated that he was alert and should have been able to operate his train in accordance with operating rules. But evidence gathered during the investigation suggests that, temporarily at least, the engineer was more attentive to his text messaging and to his anticipated meeting later that evening with young rail fans than he was to the safe operation of his train. The engineer's deficient performance reinforces the research findings that, in operational settings such as this, text messaging can lead to performance decrements related to distraction and inattention.[64] The NTSB concludes that the engineer of train 111 was actively, if intermittently, using his wireless device shortly after his train departed Chatsworth station, and his text messaging activity during this time compromised his ability to observe and appropriately respond to the *stop* signal at CP Topanga.

---

[62] J. D. Lee. (2007). "Driver Distraction: Breakdowns of a Multi-Level Control Process," In: I. J. Faulks, M. Regan, M. Stevenson, J. Brown, A. Porter & J.D. Irwin (Eds.). *Distracted Driving* (Sydney, NSW: Australasian College of Road Safety, 2007). Pp. 75-98.

[63] J. D. Hoffman, J. D. Lee, D. V. McGehee, Department of Mechanical and Industrial Engineering, Public Policy Center, The University of Iowa, Iowa City, IA. In: *Proceedings of the Human Factors and Ergonomics Society 50thAnnual Meeting, 2006.*

[64] Studies of the perceptual phenomenon known as "inattentional blindness" have demonstrated that distracted viewers can fail to detect critical visual stimuli even when they are fixating on those stimuli. See A. Mack and I. Rock. *Inattentional Blindness* (Cambridge, MA: MIT Press, 1998) for a complete discussion of the topic.

Train 111 Engineer's Use of Wireless Device

The investigation revealed that, between about 6:05 a.m. and 4:22 p.m. on the day of the accident, the engineer sent or received a total of 95 text messages. During the time periods (morning and evening shifts) that he was responsible for operating a train, he sent 21 text messages, received 20 text messages, and made four outgoing telephone calls. The investigation further revealed that this amount of activity was not unusual for this engineer. Wireless records for the 7 days preceding the accident showed that on each workday, the engineer had sent or received text messages or made voice calls during the time he was responsible for operating a train. On the day with the least wireless activity, he sent or received (during his work period) about 30 text messages. On Wednesday, 2 days before the accident, he sent or received about 125 messages during the time he was responsible for operating a train. He had also made phone calls during these periods.

The *General Code of Operating Rules* and Connex operating rules forbid non-work-related and non-emergency use of personal wireless devices by operating crewmembers. In fact, the train 111 engineer was in violation of Connex operating rules simply by having his wireless device in the locomotive cab and turned on while he was at the controls of the locomotive or cab control car. But the engineer went further, from simply having the device to actually using it to read and compose messages during the time his primary task was to operate the train safely and to be attentive and properly responsive to all signal indications.

The engineer was well aware that he was violating company rules with regard to his use of a wireless device. In 2006, as part of an efficiency test, he was found to have his cell phone turned on in his briefcase. He said that he had forgotten to turn it off when he went on duty, but he was documented at that time as having failed to comply with company safety rules. Only about a month before the accident, the conductor on the engineer's train saw the engineer using his cell phone, and he reminded him of the prohibition. The conductor said the engineer acknowledged that such use was a violation of company rules. The conductor reported the incident to a supervisor who, according to testimony during the public hearing on this accident, once again counseled the engineer with regard to the rule regarding use of wireless devices. The NTSB concludes that the Metrolink engineer was aware that he was violating company safety rules when he used his cell phone to make calls or to send and receive text messages while on duty, but he continued the practice nonetheless.

Leesdale Local Conductor's Use of Wireless Device

The engineer of train 111 was not the only crewmember involved in this accident to have made prohibited use of a wireless device. The records indicate that the conductor of the Leesdale Local sent or received a total of 41 text messages while on duty, with 35 of these being sent or received during the time the conductor's report shows that the train was moving. His last outgoing text message was received and logged by the Verizon network at 4:20 p.m., about the time his train exited tunnel 27 and about 2 minutes before the collision.

Although the conductor was in the cab of the locomotive at the time he sent his last text message before the accident, he was not at the controls. And although he, along with the engineer, was responsible for observing signal indications and helping ensure compliance with those indications, no evidence was found to indicate that the train handling of the Leesdale Local was unusual or inconsistent with the signal indications the train was operating under. The NTSB therefore concludes that, although the conductor of the Leesdale Local violated operating rules by sending and receiving text messages during times when he shared responsibility for the safe operations of his train, any distraction caused by such use did not cause or contribute to this accident.

Unauthorized Persons in Locomotive Cab

The prohibition against cell phone use was not the only company safety rule the engineer of train 111 knowingly violated. As was clear from the content of the text messages the engineer exchanged with the young rail fan identified in this report as "Person A," the engineer had, earlier in the week, allowed Person A and one or more friends to board his train and join him in the locomotive cab. The engineer apparently had allowed at least one of these individuals to operate the train for a portion of the trip. On the day of the accident, the engineer planned to have Person A and one or more other individuals board the locomotive at Moorpark. He further planned to allow Person A and perhaps one or more other individuals to actually operate the train from Moorpark to the end of the line at Montalvo. This plan was only about 3 1/2 hours from fruition when the accident occurred.

As with wireless devices, Connex had specific rules prohibiting unauthorized persons from occupying the locomotive cab or operating compartment of a train while the train was in service. The engineer was obviously aware of the rules because he conspired with the rail fans to have them board his train surreptitiously. Many of the text messages the engineer exchanged with Person A on the afternoon of the accident had to do with the planned boarding at Moorpark, with several comments reflecting full awareness, by both parties, that allowing unauthorized persons to board the train, not to mention actually operating it, constituted a violation of railroad rules.

Efficiency Testing and Management Oversight

The engineer of train 111 had been subject to efficiency and rules testing throughout his railroad career. Nothing exceptional was found in the records of this testing. As already noted, on two occasions in the previous 2 years he had been counseled about his use of a cell phone while on duty, but neither instance suggested a pattern of violations or an ongoing, willful disregard for the rules. And yet, as shown by his wireless account records (which would not have been available to Connex managers), the engineer habitually used his cell phone at times when he knew that any distraction from the task at hand could have serious safety consequences. Further, by actively encouraging and facilitating access by unauthorized persons to the locomotive cab, he created a situation that could pose another serious safety risk.

As acknowledged during the public hearing on this accident, the nature of rail operations makes enforcement of certain operating rules extremely difficult, if not impossible. Metrolink trains, as is common with other passenger trains, have only the engineer in the operating compartment. No reasonable method exists for management, by personal observation, to determine whether the engineer (or other crewmember) boards the train with a personal wireless device in his or her possession, and once the train leaves a station, no mechanism is currently in place to determine whether the device is in use.

The conductor on train 111, who 1 month before the accident had cautioned the engineer about his use of his cell phone while on duty and had taken the extra step of reporting the incident to a manager, stated that he believed this to be an isolated event and that he was not aware of the engineer's pattern of cell phone use while on duty. The engineer clearly took advantage of the privacy afforded by the locked locomotive cab to freely and repeatedly use his cell phone in violation of railroad operating rules. Even though this engineer and conductor had worked together 5 days a week, two shifts per day, for the previous 5 months, the conductor was not aware of the extent to which the engineer was using his wireless device while aboard the train. It is therefore unlikely that routine efficiency testing would ever have identified the scope of the engineer's violations with regard to wireless devices.

Similarly, the engineer's permitting of unauthorized persons to occupy the operating compartment of his locomotive stood a very low likelihood of being discovered through ordinary management supervision or efficiency testing. The engineer was familiar enough with his route and with the scope of management's oversight to be able to violate the rules without discovery. He had already allowed his rail fan friends one "ride-along" earlier in the week, and he knew where, when, and how they could again board his train undetected on the evening of the accident.

After the accident, Metrolink stiffened the penalty for unauthorized use of wireless devices by crewmembers on moving trains. Such violations will now result in immediate termination of employment. Similarly, with the issuance of Emergency Order 26, the FRA has raised violations involving the use of wireless devices to the Federal level. But making the violation more serious or the penalty more severe does not address the difficulty in identifying violators. With regard to both cell phone use and allowing unauthorized persons into his train's operating compartment, the train 111 engineer obviously had a high degree of confidence that his actions would not be detected. He already faced the prospect of severe penalties if he was caught, especially with regard to having unauthorized persons aboard, but that threat was not sufficient to deter him, given the low likelihood of detection.

As shown in the case of the conductor of the Leesdale Local, who also made inappropriate use of a wireless device to send a text message only minutes before the collision, even having other crewmembers present is an insufficient deterrent against such use.

The NTSB therefore concludes that, because of the privacy afforded by a locomotive cab or train operating compartment, routine efficiency testing and performance monitoring practices are inadequate to determine whether or to what extent engineers or other crewmembers may not be complying with safety rules such as those regarding use of wireless devices or allowing access by unauthorized persons.

In-Cab Audio and Image Recording Devices

The engineer in this accident was able to conceal his inappropriate behavior because he was aware each time he was, or could have been, observed by management. He would likely have been deterred in his cell phone use and in his allowing access to unauthorized persons only if he had known that his performance at the train controls was subject to review at any time, not just when a manager was in the operating compartment or nearby. The NTSB believes that the only reasonable and reliable mechanism for making such observations is an in-cab audio and image recorder that will capture a crewmember's activities while in the train operating compartment.

The NTSB has long supported the installation of audio recording devices in locomotive cabs or train operating compartments. In all too many accidents, the individuals directly involved are either limited in their recollection of events or, as in the case of the Chatsworth accident, are not available to be interviewed because of fatal injuries. In a number of accidents the NTSB has investigated, a better knowledge of crewmembers' actions before an accident would have helped reveal the key causal factors and would perhaps have facilitated the development of more effective safety recommendations.

As a result of its investigation of the collision between a Maryland Rail Commuter train and an Amtrak train near Silver Spring, Maryland, on February 16, 1996,[65] in which no operating crewmembers survived, the NTSB was unable to determine whether certain crewmember activities leading up to the accident may have contributed to the accident. Consequently, the NTSB recommended that the FRA:

R-97-9
Amend 49 *Code of Federal Regulations* Part 229 to require the recording of train crewmembers' voice communications for exclusive use in accident investigations and with appropriate limitations on the public release of such recordings.

After its investigation of another railroad accident with no surviving crewmembers that occurred in 1999 in Bryan, Ohio,[66] the NTSB reiterated Safety Recommendation R-97-9 to the FRA. The FRA responded that it

has reluctantly come to the conclusion that this recommendation should not be implemented at the present time. . . . FRA appreciates that, as time passes and other uses are found for recording media that may create synergies with other public and private purposes, the Board's recommendation may warrant re-examination.

Based on this response and further meetings, the NTSB classified Safety Recommendation R-97-9 "Closed—Unacceptable Action."

---

[65] Collision and Derailment of Maryland Rail Commuter MARC Train 286 and National Railroad Passenger Corporation Amtrak Train 29 Near Silver Spring, Maryland, on February 16, 1996, Railroad Accident Report NTSB/RAR-97/02 (Washington, DC: National Transportation Safety Board, 1997).

[66] *Collision Involving Three Consolidated Rail Corporation Freight Trains Operating in Fog on a Double Main Track Near Bryan, Ohio, January 17, 1999*, Railroad Accident Report NTSB/RAR-01/01 (Washington, DC: National Transportation Safety Board, 2001).

Since the refusal by the FRA to act on the recommendation regarding in-cab recorders, the NTSB has continued to investigate accidents in which such recorders would have provided valuable information to help determine probable cause and develop safety recommendations. Most recently, as a result of its investigation of a July 10, 2005, collision of two CN freight trains in Anding, Mississippi,[67] the NTSB made the following safety recommendation to the FRA:

R-07-3
Require the installation of a crash- and fire-protected locomotive cab voice recorder, or a combined voice and video recorder, (for the exclusive use in accident investigations and with appropriate limitations on the public release of such recordings) in all controlling locomotive cabs and cab car operating compartments. The recorder should have a minimum 2-hour continuous recording capability, microphones capable of capturing crewmembers' voices and sounds generated within the cab, and a channel to record all radio conversations to and from crewmembers.

Investigators in those transportation modes where such recordings are available have not only been able to analyze voice communication between operating crewmembers in the moments leading up to an accident, but they have also been able to review and analyze other sounds originating from the vehicle. From such sounds, parameters such as engine rpm, system failures, speed, and the time at which certain events occur can often be determined, leading to more precise findings and determination of probable cause. The FRA indicated in its response to the NTSB's recommendation that the subject of in-cab video and audio recordings had been discussed at a meeting of the Railroad Safety Advisory Committee Locomotive Working Group. Pending more information about those discussions, Safety Recommendation R-07-3 was classified "Open—Acceptable Response" on July 31, 2009.

As is clear from the wording of Safety Recommendations R-97-9 and R-07-3, the NTSB's emphasis up to this point has been on the use of audio and/or image recordings as a tool of accident investigation. But this accident demonstrates that audio-only in-cab recordings that may be reviewed only after an accident do not represent the most effective use of recorder technology for accident prevention. Even had the Metrolink locomotive in this accident been equipped with audio recording devices, the Metrolink engineer, with the appropriate settings on his wireless device, would most likely have been able to continue with his text messaging activities without the equipment having captured it.

The presence, in addition to audio recording capability, of in-cab image recording capability would have been the only means available to have determined exactly what actions the engineer was taking during the accident trip. These images would have revealed the engineer's text messaging activities even absent any sounds that could have been captured by an audio recorder. Similarly, any entry into the locomotive or train operating compartment by unauthorized persons would be evident on image recorders.

In accidents or incidents in which employee misbehavior is not a factor, in-cab audio and video recordings could be used to validate train crew performance as well as identify potential

---

[67] *Collision of Two CN Freight Trains, Anding, Mississippi, July 10, 2005*, Railroad Accident Report NTSB/RAR-07/01 (Washington, DC: National Transportation Safety Board, 2007).

causal or contributory system design deficiencies or equipment malfunctions that may not evident from other available parametric data.

Some railroads have already installed one type of image recorder—a forward facing video recorder—on their locomotives, primarily for use after grade crossing accidents. The two locomotives of the Leesdale Local were equipped with forward-facing video recorders. The output of those recorders was used in this accident investigation to validate the information drawn from signal data records. Although other evidence in this accident was sufficient to show conclusively that the engineer failed to comply with a red signal, forward-facing image and audio recorders can often be helpful in determining not only signal aspect, but also signal visibility, as well as identifying other external factors that may influence a train crew's performance in the period leading up to an accident.

But even if audio and video recording devices had been installed in the Metrolink train 111 locomotive before this accident, they would not have contributed to preventing it so long as their output could be used only after the accident occurred. The NTSB believes that the recorded audio and images should be easily recoverable and available for review not only after an accident has occurred but routinely, as part of the railroad's efficiency testing and performance monitoring program.[68] In the same way that operating employees are continually tested on signal compliance or speed control, audio and image recordings of engineers and other crewmembers could be reviewed at random to verify compliance with safety rules and procedures. In particular, this information could allow railroads to identify unsafe behaviors and pursue corrective action before an accident occurs. Further, an employee who is aware that his or her activities in the train control compartment are subject to review by management will be much less likely to engage in conduct—such as using a wireless device or allowing unauthorized persons in the locomotive cab—that could lead to an accident. Even if an employee is not discouraged from performing these or other unsafe acts, detection of those behaviors would prompt corrective actions that would improve safety. Additionally, not all actions or conditions that have safety implications involve employee misconduct or rules violations. Regular review of in-cab audio and image recordings would give managers insight into other potential safety issues or unsafe operating practices that may not be revealed by any other means and of which the crews themselves may be unaware. Action could then be taken to address these issues through changes in rules, operating practices, or employee training programs.

The NTSB therefore concludes that a train crew performance monitoring program that includes the use of in-cab audio and image recordings would serve as a significant deterrent to the types of noncompliance practices with safety rules engaged in by the Metrolink engineer and the UP Leesdale Local conductor in this accident and would provide railroads with a more comprehensive means to evaluate the adequacy of their safety programs.

To be effective, any such recording devices must be capable of capturing crewmember activities during a wide range of operating conditions and over a considerable period of time. The image recorders should have a resolution and frame rate sufficient to capture crew movements under typical operating conditions, which includes daylight, night, and conditions of

---

[68] As detailed in appendix B, the NTSB has, in all transportation modes, long advocated the use of recorded data not only for accident investigation, but also for safety management and employee oversight.

varying sun angles.[69] The duration of the recording should be at least 12 hours. Railroad crewmembers may be on duty for up to 12 hours, and their actions or inactions at any time during that period could set the stage for an accident. Also, from the standpoint of efficiency testing or performance monitoring, the more information that is available to management, the more likely it is that the company can assess the performance of its people or the effectiveness of its training.

The NTSB therefore recommends that the FRA require the installation, in all controlling locomotive cabs and cab car operating compartments, of crash- and fire-protected inward- and outward-facing audio and image recorders capable of providing recordings to verify that train crew actions are in accordance with rules and procedures that are essential to safety as well as train operating conditions. The devices should have a minimum 12-hour continuous recording capability with recordings that are easily accessible for review, with appropriate limitations on public release, for the investigation of accidents or for use by management in carrying out efficiency testing and systemwide performance monitoring programs. Because this recommendation expands upon and reinforces the intent of Safety Recommendation R-07-3, that recommendation is reclassified "Closed—Unacceptable Action/Superseded."

If image and audio recordings are to be used to prevent, and not simply to reconstruct, accidents, railroad managers must be authorized to review the recordings regularly as part of their programs of efficiency testing and performance monitoring of train crews. The NTSB therefore recommends that the FRA require that railroads regularly review and use in-cab audio and image recordings (with appropriate limitations on public release), in conjunction with other performance data, to verify that train crew actions are in accordance with rules and procedures that are essential to safety.

Concerns about individual privacy have typically influenced decisions about the installation and use of audio or image recorders to record crewmembers at work. However, the NTSB does not believe that employee privacy should take precedence over public safety given the many accidents and incidents, in all transportation modes, that the NTSB has investigated that involved vehicle operator distraction. Workers in safety-critical positions in all industries should expect to be observed in the workplace, just as most employees should expect their employers to be able to monitor such activities as e-mail and Web browsing during work hours. The argument for complete privacy in settings such as a locomotive cab, where lives of many are entrusted to the care of one, is not persuasive.

The NTSB notes that, since the accident, SCRRA has installed inward- and forward-facing cameras in its Metrolink locomotives to monitor engineer compliance with rules regarding electronic devices, unauthorized personnel, and sleeping on duty.

---

[69] International specifications for aircraft accident investigation recorders state a minimum frame rate of 4 images per second and overall resolution sufficient to distinguish between parallel 5mm resolution bars on a standard image resolution chart. Source: *Minimum Operational Performance Specification for Crash Protected Airborne Recorder Systems, ED-112* (Paris: The European Organisation for Civil Aviation Equipment, 2003).

Metrolink Passenger Survivability

For those passengers in the first coach who were in the section of the railcar that was subject to the telescoping action, the accident was generally not survivable. For those passengers who were occupying the area just behind the telescoped section but in front of the rear vestibule/stairwell area, the accident was borderline survivable, although most of those individuals who survived sustained injuries either because of the deceleration forces or from interaction with elements of the car that were crushed. For those passengers occupying the section of the first railcar that was not subject to the telescoping action (that is, the part aft of the rear vestibule/stairwell), the risk of injury came from the substantial deceleration forces that their bodies absorbed.

The occupants of the second and third passenger coaches experienced essentially no loss of occupant survival space, but they, too, were at risk of injury from deceleration forces. The magnitude of these forces decreased with distance from the point of impact. The NTSB concludes that passenger survivability in this accident was determined almost exclusively by where an individual was located, and the extremely high collision forces resulted in a loss of occupant survival space in the forward two-thirds of the first passenger coach.

For the type of passenger coach involved in this accident, the FRA has issued minimum static end-loading strength and crashworthiness requirements. Based on documentation reviewed as part of this accident investigation, the design of the BiLevel railcars involved in this accident was in compliance with FRA regulatory requirements. Also, during the physical inspection of the damaged equipment and subsequent review of FRA compliance certification documentation, nothing was found to suggest that the coaches were not built to FRA standards.

The NTSB does have a concern, however, about the workstation tables that are situated throughout the BiLevel coaches. These tables (four tables on the upper level and two at each intermediate level) are fitted between paired sets of passenger seats. As configured, these one-piece tabletops are at abdomen height for a passenger seated at the table, thus placing that person at risk of sustaining serious abdominal injury in the event of a high-g deceleration (such as a collision impact).

As a result of its investigation of the 2002 collision of a Metrolink commuter train with a Burlington Northern Santa Fe freight train in Placentia, California,[70] the NTSB determined that two Metrolink passengers had been fatally injured as a result of abdominal injuries resulting from impact with a workstation table. The investigation also identified research undertaken by the FRA, using resources of the Volpe National Transportation Systems Center and other organizations, to address collision-induced injury resulting from these workstation tables. This research has resulted in some prototype designs for further evaluation. In the meantime, SCRRA has indicated to the NTSB that it is purchasing Crash Energy Management cab control cars and trailer cars that will be placed in operation starting in 2010. These cars will have crash-energy seats, frangible tables, and push-back couplers. Existing Metrolink coaches will also be retrofitted with these same features. The NTSB is encouraged by the progress being made in this

---

[70] *Collision of Burlington Northern Santa Fe Freight Train With Metrolink Passenger Train, Placentia, California, April 23, 2002,* Railroad Accident Report NTSB/RAR-03/04 (Washington, DC: National Transportation Safety Board, 2003).

area by the FRA, SCRAA, and others and will continue to monitor developments that reduce the risk of injury and death to rail passengers during an accident.

Positive Train Control

The accident at Chatsworth was the second accident involving a collision between a freight train and a Metrolink passenger train that the NTSB has investigated. In the previously referenced investigation into the 2002 collision in Placentia, California, the NTSB determined that the eastbound Burlington Northern Santa Fe freight train failed to comply with an *approach* signal indication and was therefore unable to stop short of the next signal, which was displaying a *stop* indication. The train continued past the *stop* signal and collided head-on with a Metrolink passenger train. The accident resulted in 2 fatalities and more than 100 injuries.

The NTSB has long advocated the implementation of positive train control systems that would prevent train-to-train collisions such as those that occurred at Placentia and Chatsworth. Over the past 4 decades, the NTSB has investigated a multitude of railroad accidents that could have been avoided through use of a positive train control system that will automatically assume some control of a train if the crew does not comply with a signal indication. The NTSB concludes that had a fully implemented positive train control system been in place on the Ventura Subdivision at the time of this accident, it would have intervened to stop Metrolink train 111 before the engineer could pass the red signal at CP Topanga, and the collision would not have occurred.

Positive train control was on the NTSB's Most Wanted List of Transportation Safety Improvements since the list's inception in 1990. The NTSB's many investigations of train collisions have resulted in the issuance of a number of safety recommendations, the most recent of which was issued as a result of the investigation of a collision involving three freight trains in Bryan, Ohio.[71] That recommendation, issued to the FRA, was as follows:

R-01-6
Facilitate actions necessary for development and implementation of positive train control systems that include collision avoidance, and require implementation of positive train control systems on main line tracks, establishing priority requirements for high-risk corridors such as those where commuter and intercity passenger railroads operate.

In its report on the 2002 accident in Placentia, California, the NTSB reiterated Safety Recommendation R-01-6 to the FRA. While disappointed in the time that has elapsed since the issuance of the recommendation, with little effective action by the FRA, the NTSB notes that the Rail Safety Improvement Act of 2008 mandates that not later than 18 months from the date of enactment, Class I railroads shall develop and submit to the Secretary of Transportation a plan for implementing a positive train control system by December 31, 2015. The date of enactment

---

[71] *Collision Involving Three Consolidated Rail Corporation Freight Trains Operating in Fog at Bryan, Ohio, January 17, 1999*, Railroad Accident Report NTSB/RAR-01/01 (Washington, D.C.: National Transportation Safety Board, 2001).

was October 16, 2008, making the required date for submission of plans April 16, 2010. This mandate will apply to Metrolink trackage in the accident area.

The NTSB is further encouraged that SCRRA is already engaged in the development and deployment of positive train control on the Metrolink locomotive fleet by December 2012, with the installation of positive train control on the entire SCRRA territory projected for completion by 2015.

Conclusions

Findings

1. The following were neither causal nor contributory to this accident: weather, fatigue, the engineer's medical conditions or treatments, training and experience of crewmembers, operation of Union Pacific Leesdale Local, alcohol or illegal drug use by operating crewmembers, and condition of the track or rolling stock.

2. Although the conductor of the Union Pacific Leesdale Local had likely used marijuana within 3 to 11 hours of the accident, this was neither causal nor contributory to the accident.

3. Considering the challenges of the recovery operations, the emergency response to the accident was timely, well coordinated, and effectively managed.

4. Because locomotive cab exits are not designed to be quickly opened in an emergency, firefighters could not rapidly enter the cab of the Union Pacific Leesdale Local to rescue the injured crew.

5. Physical evidence, documentary and recorded data, and postaccident signal examination and testing confirm that the westbound signal at Control Point Topanga was displaying a red aspect at the time Metrolink train 111 departed Chatsworth station and as it approached and passed Control Point Topanga, and had the engineer complied with this signal indication, the accident would not have occurred.

6. Eyewitness reports of seeing a green aspect from the Chatsworth station are contrary to the other evidence; postaccident testing and research show that witnesses could not have reliably seen the red aspect that the Control Point Topanga signal was displaying as train 111 departed the station because of a combination of extreme distance to the signal (more than 1 mile), lighting conditions at the time, and limitations of the human visual system.

7. The signal and traffic control systems worked as designed on the day of the collision, and the dispatcher's "stacking" of train routes played no role in the accident.

8. The engineer of train 111 was actively, if intermittently, using his wireless device shortly after his train departed Chatsworth station, and his text messaging activity during this time compromised his ability to observe and appropriately respond to the *stop* signal at Control Point Topanga.

9. The Metrolink engineer was aware that he was violating company safety rules when he used his cell phone to make calls or to send and receive text messages while on duty, but he continued the practice nonetheless.

10. Although the conductor of the Union Pacific Leesdale Local violated operating rules by sending and receiving text messages during times when he shared responsibility for the safe operations of his train, any distraction caused by such use did not cause or contribute to this accident.

11. Because of the privacy afforded by a locomotive cab or train operating compartment, routine efficiency testing and performance monitoring practices are inadequate to determine whether or to what extent engineers or other crewmembers may not be complying with safety rules such as those regarding use of wireless devices or allowing access by unauthorized persons.

12. A train crew performance monitoring program that includes the use of in-cab audio and image recordings would serve as a significant deterrent to the types of noncompliance practices with safety rules engaged in by the Metrolink engineer and the Union Pacific Leesdale Local conductor in this accident and would provide railroads with a more comprehensive means to evaluate the adequacy of their safety programs.

13. Passenger survivability in this accident was determined almost exclusively by where an individual was located, and the extremely high collision forces resulted in a loss of occupant survival space in the forward two-thirds of the first passenger coach.

14. Had a fully implemented positive train control system been in place on the Ventura Subdivision at the time of this accident, it would have intervened to stop Metrolink train 111 before the engineer could pass the red signal at Control Point Topanga, and the collision would not have occurred.

Probable Cause

The National Transportation Safety Board determines that the probable cause of the September 12, 2008, collision of a Metrolink commuter train and a Union Pacific freight train was the failure of the Metrolink engineer to observe and appropriately respond to the red signal aspect at Control Point Topanga because he was engaged in prohibited use of a wireless device, specifically text messaging, that distracted him from his duties. Contributing to the accident was the lack of a positive train control system that would have stopped the Metrolink train short of the red signal and thus prevented the collision.

Recommendations

As a result of its investigation of the September 12, 2008, collision of Metrolink train 111 with Union Pacific LOF65–12 at Chatsworth, California, the National Transportation Safety Board makes the following safety recommendations:

New Recommendations

To the Federal Railroad Administration:

Require the installation, in all controlling locomotive cabs and cab car operating compartments, of crash- and fire-protected inward- and outward-facing audio and image recorders capable of providing recordings to verify that train crew actions are in accordance with rules and procedures that are essential to safety as well as train operating conditions. The devices should have a minimum 12-hour continuous recording capability with recordings that are easily accessible for review, with appropriate limitations on public release, for the investigation of accidents or for use by management in carrying out efficiency testing and systemwide performance monitoring programs. (R-10-1)

Require that railroads regularly review and use in-cab audio and image recordings (with appropriate limitations on public release), in conjunction with other performance data, to verify that train crew actions are in accordance with rules and procedures that are essential to safety. (R-10-2)

Previously Issued Recommendation Reclassified in This Report

To the Federal Railroad Administration:

R-07-3
Require the installation of a crash- and fire-protected locomotive cab voice recorder, or a combined voice and video recorder, (for the exclusive use in accident investigations and with appropriate limitations on the public release of such recordings) in all controlling locomotive cabs and cab car operating compartments. The recorder should have a minimum 2-hour continuous recording capability, microphones capable of capturing crewmembers' voices and sounds generated within the cab, and a channel to record all radio conversations to and from crewmembers.

Safety Recommendation R-07-3, previously classified "Open—Acceptable Response," is reclassified "Closed—Unacceptable Action/Superseded." Safety Recommendation R-07-3 is superseded by Safety Recommendation R-10-1.

BY THE NATIONAL TRANSPORTATION SAFETY BOARD

DEBORAH A.P. HERSMAN
Chairman

CHRISTOPHER A. HART
Vice Chairman

ROBERT L. SUMWALT
Member

Adopted: January 21, 2010

Chairman Hersman filed the following concurring statement and was joined by Vice Chairman Hart and Member Sumwalt.

Chairman Deborah A.P. Hersman, Concurring Statement,

Vice Chairman Christopher A. Hart and Board Member Robert L. Sumwalt, joining in:

On January 21, 2010, by a 3-0 vote, we adopted the report on the collision of a Metrolink passenger train with a Union Pacific freight train in Chatsworth, CA. This action concluded our sixteen-month investigation into the September 12, 2008, collision that took 25 lives and injured 135.

As our report concludes, the probable cause of the collision was the failure of the Metrolink engineer to comply with the red signal at Control Point Topanga because he was texting on his personal wireless device, in violation of company policy. Distracted from his duties, he did not stop the train and collided head-on with the approaching freight train. He did so, despite earlier track signals and radio calls indicating he would need to stop. Contributing to the accident was the lack of a positive train control (PTC) system that would have stopped the train short of the red signal and thus prevented the collision.

In order to protect the safety of the traveling public, we reluctantly move further in this report, in terms of reducing privacy in the train cab, than we ever have before. We recommend that the Federal Railroad Administration (FRA) require the installation of audio and video recorders in train cabs for use in accident investigations and by management in carrying out efficiency testing and performance monitoring programs, and require railroads to regularly monitor these recorders to ensure employees are following the safety rules.

Sensitive to privacy concerns, we have endeavored to respond to the inappropriate use of cell phones and other wireless devices in ways that minimize intrusions of privacy. The Safety Board's efforts in this area date back to May 2002, with an accident in Clarendon, TX, in which an engineer was using his cell phone during the time he should have been reading a track warrant notifying him to stop the train. This led to a head-on collision with an oncoming train. As a result, the Safety Board recommended that the Federal Railroad Administration (FRA) issue regulations to control the use of cell phones and similar wireless communication devices by railroad operating employees while on duty. For more than 5 years, the FRA failed to address this issue -- until one month after the Chatsworth accident when it issued an emergency order restricting the use of cell phones and other distracting electronic devices by on-duty railroad operating employees. More recently, in May of 2009, the Safety Board investigated a collision involving two trolleys in Boston, MA. The operator of the striking train admitted to local authorities that he was texting his girlfriend in the moments immediately prior to the collision. In our Chatsworth investigation, records showed that the Metrolink engineer habitually violated company policy, such as the ban on the use of cell phones while on duty. On the day of this accident, he made four outgoing phone calls while he was on duty, and he sent or received 95 text messages, 41 of which were while he was on duty, including one 22 seconds before the collision. Also contrary to company policy, the engineer actively facilitated unauthorized persons to access the locomotive cab, and on at least one occasion, even allowed a minor to take the controls. Although he had been subject to efficiency and rules testing throughout his career and been counseled by management twice on his improper cell phone use, this inappropriate behavior continued.

Meanwhile, although not contributing to the accident, the conductor of the UP train was also texting moments before the collision. These were two different employees, working for two different companies, on two different trains. Our report concluded that, among other things, because of the privacy afford by a locomotive cab, Metrolink's routine efficiency testing and performance monitoring practices were inadequate to prevent the accident engineer from engaging in inappropriate behaviors.

This is a watershed investigation for the Safety Board. Some may have concerns that the recommendations in this report are over-reaching, that they impinge upon individual privacy, and that the oversight footprint is too broad. We uniformly disagree. The Safety Board has long supported the installation of audio recording devices in locomotive cabs for investigative purposes. Recommendations regarding audio recorders in locomotive cabs have been on our Most Wanted Listed and have been closed and reissued over the years, but the FRA has not acted on these recommendations. Furthermore, what this and other accidents have shown is that traditional forms of oversight are not working.

The Safety Board's history is filled with examples where significant accidents have resulted in significant change. In the early 1980's, the Safety Board began recommending the use of drug and alcohol testing for rail personnel. However, it wasn't until two major rail accidents in the late 1980's that Congress stepped in and decided that the societal benefits of mandatory testing outweighed any privacy concerns. Similarly, the Board has been pushing for PTC, or some version of it, for over 30 years. Finally, after this accident, Congress again stepped it to pass a bill requiring railroads to install PTC systems on passenger and certain hazmat routes by the end of 2015. Sadly, it took 25 more lives and an act of Congress to finally move PTC, on passenger rail lines, from testing to reality.

Technology is a game changer - and our Chatsworth recommendations recognize this. Today, video recorders are everywhere, and we accept them. Video cameras record us at the ATM and record bank tellers at work. Whether we are in a casino in Las Vegas or at Walmart, there are cameras recording our every move. Even our Board meetings are webcast so that others may observe our work and monitor how well we are doing our job.

In transportation, we have long accepted cameras for safety, surveillance and security. In many cities, our children and their bus drivers are recorded on school buses for behavioral reasons. Airports have cameras recording activities inside and outside of the terminals. At the Safety Board, we often use video provided by airports to identify crash sequences. Trains such as the freight train involved in this accident have been equipped with outward facing cameras mounted on the locomotives to record, among other things, grade crossing accidents. Motor coaches have inward facing cameras, which we have used in our investigations to correlate driver actions, vehicle performance and evidence from the roadway. There are even cameras photographing traffic light violators.

On a daily basis, we use technology to monitor the machines - the health of the equipment, any needed maintenance, time between overhauls, and total cycles. We now have a corresponding obligation to use that technology to monitor the people operating the machines. The rail industry still relies on an extra person in the cab to monitor whether engineers are following safety rules. Because accidents such as Chatsworth are demonstrating not only that prohibitions have not been effective, but that monitoring the prohibitions has also not been effective, we can, and must, exploit technological advances in equipment and communications to remedy this.

The Safety Board is an independent agency. Our mandate is to investigate accidents, determine their probable causes, and issue recommendations to prevent them from happening in the future. We are a safety organization, and our mission is to make transportation safer for the travelling public. We cannot, however, do this work alone. While the Safety Board can constantly raise the bar, it is incumbent upon our partners, -- industry, labor and the regulators - to take the next step and implement our recommendations.

The Safety Board's work on this accident investigation has opened a lot of eyes. What we are recommending recognizes that technology brings problems but technology also provides solutions. We did not make these recommendations lightly. In reconciling our concerns regarding privacy, we note that Congress has charged the Safety Board to identify safety deficiencies and make recommendations to improve safety. It is a responsibility that we take seriously.

Yes, it's an intrusion. Yes, it affects privacy. But when individual behaviors endanger the lives of the travelling public, we are obligated to do everything possible to ensure their safety. Just as we cannot turn a blind eye to that responsibility, however, neither can management turn a blind eye to the behavior of bad actors who are not doing their job. Management is, and must be held, accountable for the performance of their employees.

Professionalism is doing the right thing when nobody is watching. But as the Chatsworth investigation uncovered, this particular engineer was not likely to do the right thing unless he thought somebody was watching. This is a new paradigm, this area of distractions. It is changing how humans behave, how they interact with one another, and how they react in normal and emergency situations.

Our recommendations from this accident will make some people uncomfortable. They may even make some people angry. But it is not the Safety Board's job to recommend the easy things. It is the Safety Board's job to be a catalyst for change and to raise the bar. If we are serious about addressing distractions in the operating environment and serious about putting safety first, then we must put the collective ahead of the individual. We believe our recommendations are a step in that direction.

Appendix A: Investigation

Notification

The National Response Center notified the NTSB of the accident about 7:45 p.m. on September 12, 2008. The investigator-in-charge and other members of the NTSB investigative team were launched from the Washington, D.C., headquarters office and from the Chicago, Illinois; Gardena, California; and Jacksonville, Florida; field offices. The NTSB's investigation focused on all aspects of the accident, including operations, track, signals, mechanical, human performance, survival factors, crashworthiness, event recorder, and cellular telephone issues. The on-scene investigation was completed on September 20, 2008.

Member Kathryn O'Leary Higgins was the Board Member on scene. Safety Board investigators returned to the Chatsworth, California, area for follow-on investigative activities during October and November 2008 and January 2009.

Parties to the Investigation

Participating in the investigation were the FRA, Metrolink, Connex Railroad, LLC, Union Pacific Railroad, California Public Utilities Commission, Brotherhood of Locomotive Engineers and Trainmen, United Transportation Union, Los Angeles Police Department, Los Angeles Fire and Rescue, Bombardier Transportation Corporation, and Mass Electric Construction Company.

Public hearing

A public hearing on this accident was held at the NTSB Conference Center on March 3–4, 2009. Representatives of all parties to the investigation participated in the hearing.

Appendix B: Recommendation History on Employee Performance Monitoring

The NTSB has, in rail[72] as well as in other modes of transportation, long advocated the use of recorded data not only for accident investigation, but also for safety management and employee oversight. For example, in its investigation of the November 6, 1993, collision of the passenger ship *Noordam* with the Maltese bulk carrier *Mount Ymitos* near the entrance to the Mississippi River,[73] the NTSB found deficiencies in bridge watchstanding. As a result, the NTSB recommended that the U.S. Coast Guard require the installation of voyage event recorders (VERs) on all vessels over 1,600 gross tons operating in U.S. waters (Safety Recommendations M-95-5 and -6). The NTSB noted that, when used for management oversight, VERs (also known as voyage data recorders, or VDRs) would help prevent accidents, and that when used for accident reconstruction, VERs would help investigators determine what measures will promote greater safety in the future.

In its investigation of the July 16, 2004, multi-vehicle accident near Chelsea, Michigan,[74] the NTSB found that the accident was initiated when the driver of a tractor-semitrailer combination failed to stop upon encountering traffic congestion in a temporary traffic control zone, likely due to reduced alertness because of a failure to obtain adequate rest. The driver's hours of service at the time of the accident exceeded Federal limits by 5.75 hours. Contributing to the accident were motor carrier's insufficient regard for, and oversight of, driver compliance with Federal hours-of-service regulations, and the failure of the Federal Motor Carrier Safety Administration's (FMCSA) to require motor carriers to use tamperproof driver's logs. In its investigation of the accident, the Safety Board determined that data from the electronic on-board recorder (EOBR) in the accident tractor were instrumental in the reconstruction of events leading to the accident and in the assessment of the accident driver's hours-of-service status. Because of the value of these data and the deficiencies identified in the FMCSA's hours-of-service compliance review program, the NTSB concluded that carriers should use EOBRs to verify compliance for all operators subject to hours-of-service regulations. Therefore, in 2007, the NTSB recommended that the FMCSA require all interstate commercial vehicle carriers to use EOBRs so that the carriers and their regulators could monitor and assess hours-of-service compliance (Safety Recommendation H-07-41).

The NTSB's investigation into a number of aviation accidents also prompted recommendations related to the use of accident recorders for operational oversight by safety managers. For example, in its investigation of the October 14, 2004, crash of Pinnacle Airlines

---

[72] For example, see NTSB Safety Recommendations R-81-65, R-81-67, R-84-38, R-87-21, and R-90-17.

[73] *Collision of the Netherlands Antilles Passenger Ship* Noordam *and the Maltese Bulk Carrier* Mount Ymitos *in the Gulf of Mexico November 6, 1993*, Marine Accident Report NTSB/Mar-95/01 (Washington, DC: National Transportation Safety Board, 1995).

[74] *Rear-End Chain Reaction Collision, Interstate 94 East, Near Chelsea, Michigan, July 16, 2004*, Highway Accident Brief NTSB/HAB-07/01 (Washington, DC: National Transportation Safety Board, 2007).

flight 3407 near Jefferson City, Missouri,[75] the NTSB found repeated instances of unprofessional conduct by flight crews during repositioning flights when no passengers or cabin attendants were on board. This behavior occurred for a number of reasons, including the crews' perception of a low risk of detection. As a result, the NTSB recommended that the Federal Aviation Administration require those regional air carriers having the capability to review flight data recorder data from nonrevenue flights to use that data to verify that flights are being conducted in accordance with standard operating procedures (Safety Recommendation A-07-7).

Most recently, the NTSB noted that a flight operations monitoring program, had it been in place, may have helped prevent the collision of two helicopters carrying out helicopter emergency medical services flights in Flagstaff, Arizona, on June 29, 2008. The two Bell 407 helicopters collided in midair while approaching the Flagstaff Medical Center helipad. The NTSB determined that the probable cause of this accident was that the two pilots failed to see and avoid each other as their aircraft approached the helipad. Contributing to the accident were the failure of one of the pilots to follow arrival and noise abatement guidelines and the failure of the other pilot to follow communication guidelines. The NTSB concluded that the systematic monitoring of data from helicopter emergency medical services flights could provide operators with objective information regarding the manner in which their pilots are conducting these flights. The NTSB further concluded that a periodic review of such information, along with other available information such as pilot reports and medical crew feedback, could assist operators in detecting and correcting unsafe deviations from company operating procedures. As a result, the NTSB recommended that the FAA require helicopter emergency medical services flight operators to install flight data recording devices and establish a structured flight data management program that reviews all available data sources to identify deviations from established norms and procedures and other potential safety issues (Safety Recommendation A-09-90).

---

[75] *Crash of Pinnacle Airlines Flight 3701, Bombardier CL-600-2B19, N8396A, Jefferson City, Missouri, October 14, 2004,* Aircraft Accident Report NTSB/AAR-07/01 (Washington, DC: National Transportation Safety Board, 1995).